Human Tr... in Ohio

Markets, Responses, and Considerations

Jeremy M. Wilson, Erin Dalton

Supported by the Ohio Association of Chiefs of Police

Safety and Justice

A RAND INFRASTRUCTURE, SAFETY, AND ENVIRONMENT PROGRAM

The research described in this report was supported by a grant awarded by the Office of Justice Programs, through the State of Ohio, Office of Criminal Justice Services, in a grant provided to the Ohio Association of Chiefs of Police and was conducted under the auspices of the Safety and Justice Program within RAND Infrastructure, Safety, and Environment (ISE).

Library of Congress Cataloging-in-Publication Data

Wilson, Jeremy M., 1974–
    Human trafficking in Ohio : markets, responses, and considerations / Jeremy M. Wilson, Erin Dalton.
        p. cm.
    Includes bibliographical references.
    ISBN 978-0-8330-4296-5 (pbk. : alk. paper)
    1. Human trafficking—Ohio. 2. Human trafficking—Government policy—Ohio. 3. Forced labor—Prevention. I. Dalton, Erin. II. Title.

HQ281.W55 2007
364.15—dc22

                                                                    2007040787

The RAND Corporation is a nonprofit research organization providing objective analysis and effective solutions that address the challenges facing the public and private sectors around the world. RAND's publications do not necessarily reflect the opinions of its research clients and sponsors.

RAND® is a registered trademark.

Published 2007 by the RAND Corporation
1776 Main Street, P.O. Box 2138, Santa Monica, CA 90407-2138
1200 South Hayes Street, Arlington, VA 22202-5050
4570 Fifth Avenue, Suite 600, Pittsburgh, PA 15213-2665
RAND URL: http://www.rand.org/
To order RAND documents or to obtain additional information, contact
Distribution Services: Telephone: (310) 451-7002;
Fax: (310) 451-6915; Email: order@rand.org

Preface

Although human trafficking—both sex and labor trafficking—is a growing national (and global) concern, it is ultimately a problem that will be identified at the local level. Ohio has several characteristics that some speculate may make it conducive to sex and labor trafficking. Media attention to prominent interstate cases involving teen prostitutes recruited from Toledo further fuel this fear. Yet, aside from various anecdotal accounts, there is little knowledge about trafficking in Ohio.

This monograph is designed to provide context about human trafficking in Ohio to help inform and shape public discourse and practical responses to it. To do so, it systematically explores human trafficking in terms of its existence and characteristics and in terms of how the criminal justice and social service communities have responded to it. The goal is to provide policymakers and practitioners with information to help improve their efforts to protect and provide services to victims and to bring perpetrators to justice. This monograph will also be of value to legislators and practitioners in other states who are concerned about this issue, as well as to researchers who are seeking to better understand human trafficking and the social response to it.

This project was supported by a grant awarded by the Office of Justice Programs, through the State of Ohio, Office of Criminal Justice Services, in a grant provided to the Ohio Association of Chiefs of Police. The opinions, findings, conclusions, and recommendations expressed in this publication are those of the authors and do not necessarily reflect the views of the Department of Justice, the Ohio Association of Chiefs of Police, or the State of Ohio, Office of Criminal Justice Services.

Those who read this monograph may also find interest in some of RAND's other recent publications that focus on issues of concern in Ohio:

- Greg Ridgeway, Terry Schell, K. Jack Riley, Susan Turner, and Travis L. Dixon, *Police-Community Relations in Cincinnati: Year Two Evaluation Report* (TR-445-CC), 2006
- K. Jack Riley, Susan Turner, John MacDonald, Greg Ridgeway, Terry Schell, Jeremy M. Wilson, Travis L. Dixon, Terry Fain, Dionne Barnes-Proby, and Brent D. Fulton, *Police-Community Relations in Cincinnati* (TR-333-CC), 2005
- Roland Sturm, William Goldman, and Joyce McCulloch, "Mental Health and Substance Abuse Parity: A Case Study of Ohio's State Employee Program" (RP-754), 1999
- "Federal Research and Development in Ohio," in Donna Fossum, Lawrence S. Painter, Valerie L. Williams, Allison Yezril, Elaine M. Newton, David Trinkle, *Discovery and Innovation: Federal Research and Development Activities in the Fifty States, District of Columbia, and Puerto Rico* (MR-1194-OSTP/NSF), 2000, pp. 421–436.

The RAND Safety and Justice Program

This research was conducted under the auspices of the Safety and Justice Program within RAND Infrastructure, Safety, and Environment (ISE). The mission of RAND ISE is to improve the development, operation, use, and protection of society's essential physical assets and natural resources and to enhance the related social assets of safety and security of individuals in transit and in their workplaces and communities. Safety and Justice Program research addresses occupational safety, transportation safety, food safety, and public safety—including violence, policing, corrections, substance abuse, and public integrity.

Questions or comments about this monograph should be sent to the project leader, Jeremy Wilson (Jeremy_Wilson@rand.org). Information about the Safety and Justice Program is available online (http://www.rand.org/ise/safety). Inquiries about research projects should be sent to the following address:

Andrew Morral, Director
Safety and Justice Program, ISE
RAND Corporation
1200 South Hayes Street
Arlington, VA 22202-5050
703-413-1100, x5119
Andrew_Morral@rand.org

Contents

Tables

Summary

Introduction

Fueled partly by media attention, there has been a growing focus on human trafficking in the United States, a focus that has grown significantly in the past decade. In the United States, this growing interest culminated in the passage of the Trafficking Victims Protection Act (TVPA), which was signed into law in October 2000. This act and its subsequent 2003 and 2005 reauthorizations are the main tools used in combating both domestic and worldwide human trafficking.

The growing interest in human trafficking has also spurred an interest in research. Unfortunately, existing research on human trafficking has yet to move the field beyond estimating the scale of the problem; mapping relationships among origin, transport, and destination countries; and analyzing policy responses to it. Such research is limited by a lack of consensus on the definition of *human trafficking* and by the operationalization of that definition, by the nature of the population itself, and by the difficulty of determining how to count human-trafficking victims. Given these problems, much of the existing research on trafficking attempts to show that it is a problem and to give a snapshot of that problem by relying on overviews, commentaries, and anecdotal information.

This assessment explores the existence and characteristics of human trafficking in Ohio, with a focus on the extent to which human trafficking occurs (its existence), characteristics (limited to concrete cases for which there is evidence supporting a trafficking offense), and the awareness and response of the criminal justice and social service communities to human trafficking. The study examines two urban communities—Columbus and Toledo—to explore the characteristics of and response to human trafficking in Ohio, relying on a content analysis of newspaper accounts and key respondent interviews with criminal justice officials and social service providers in each site.

Existence of Human Trafficking in Case Study Sites

Focusing on concrete cases identified in the content analysis (January 2003 through June 2006) and in the interviews (February through July 2007), we identified 15 cases in the two case study sites. Our identification of concrete cases should be interpreted as a minimum baseline or lower-bound estimate of human trafficking. Although there are few identified cases relative to other crimes, most respondents believe that the problem is significantly larger than they know of: Some suggested that there are as many as three to 10 trafficking victims of this type for every one identified. There are dozens of traffickers currently under investigation in one of the case study sites, and there is some evidence that the size of the problem may be increasing or may have increased in recent years. For example, one respondent suggested that, as recently as the 1980s, it was against all norms to involve a child in prostitution; today, it is the norm, within prostitution rings. However, many respondents felt that the issue has always existed but that there is increased awareness of it today.

There were two types of human-trafficking markets identified in the case study sites. The first trafficking market centered on juvenile prostitution, which numerous newspaper articles and respondents in Toledo identified. Respondents identified this market in Columbus, although they could not provide any specific case information. The second trafficking market centered on labor, which was not found in Toledo but was identified by four respondents (representing two agencies) in Columbus. Given the small number of cases, there is very little basis for comparison between the two sites.

Justice System Response in Case Study Sites

Columbus and Toledo have considerably different responses to juvenile sex-trafficking cases. In Columbus, there is almost no awareness that human trafficking can involve juveniles in commercial sex transactions from which an adult benefits. This lack of awareness, coupled with lack of resources, lack of local and federal law enforcement collaboration, lack of dedicated staff or a dedicated unit to handle trafficking cases, and lack of systematic community–service provider partnerships, leads to handling potential human-trafficking victims as offenders, which may partly lead to the lack of identified human-trafficking cases in the jurisdiction.

In Toledo, the criminal justice community has made significant changes to promote awareness, identification, and investigation of human-trafficking cases. Federal resources and collaborations among federal, state, and local law enforcement and service providers have helped facilitate this change. Local law enforcement respondents (n = 3) claimed that these changes have led to the increase in the number of cases investigated and prosecuted in Toledo involving Toledo-area actors.

In both Toledo and Columbus, there is a reported disconnect between the justice system's and the child welfare system's responses to juvenile sex-trafficking cases, which may hinder the identification and prosecution of cases.

Law enforcement authorities were not made aware of the few known labor-trafficking cases in Columbus, and there were no known cases in Toledo. However, law enforcement agencies in both communities suggested that they would respond to such cases if they were made aware of them.

Social Service Provider and Community Response in Case Study Sites

In Columbus, there is little identification of human-trafficking cases. As such, little response was seen by service providers or by the community, with the exception of one provider that has seen a few victims of labor exploitation. Furthermore, there is no awareness of possible juvenile sex-trafficking victims in Columbus, despite the broad consideration of the issue in Toledo. Despite this, respondents in Columbus indicated that, if they identified a human-trafficking victim, they would make partnerships and use their existing networks to serve the victim.

In Toledo, there has been a considerable reaction and response to juvenile trafficking victims by the community. While these programs are still small and struggling and may only be prepared to address juvenile victims, compared to Columbus, Toledo has an extensive, organized, and collaborative approach to dealing with human-trafficking victims.

As such, the only similarities found between the two case study sites were the need for more shelter options for victims of human trafficking and the disconnect between the child welfare and juvenile justice systems' treatment of children and families with possible connections to human trafficking.

Key Policy Considerations

Given the relatively small number of cases we identified, policymakers and practitioners must carefully weigh their response to this crime relative to other priorities. Providing resources, in whatever form, to more effectively address one type of offense necessarily limits resources that can be used to address another.

Despite the small number of concrete cases we identified, there are several factors that warrant, at a minimum, further discussion about response options. First, our identification of concrete cases should be interpreted as a minimum baseline or lower-bound estimate of human trafficking. It is possible that additional cases exist in other areas of Ohio, possibly even in Columbus and Toledo, or that cases involving victims and offenders from Ohio appear elsewhere in the United States. Second, each case can involve numerous victims and offenders (six cases currently being investigated in Toledo involve as many as 60 traffickers). Third, this offense has existed as a crime only since 2000, and changing traditional practices takes both time and training. Finally, human trafficking is a clandestine crime; directing more resources toward it and increasing awareness of it generally coincide with the identification of more cases.

If policymakers and practitioners want to improve on the current response to human trafficking, our analysis offers several suggestions:

- Improve awareness and response through training, education, and outreach.
- Improve victim programs and resources.
- Improve law enforcement capacity.
- Improve practitioner collaboration.
- Refine departmental policies.
- Use analyses to develop evidence-based programs and responses.
- Consider and assess legislative, legal, and regulatory changes.

Acknowledgments

Numerous people and organizations made this study possible and greatly enhanced the analytical process and product. We would like to thank the Ohio Office of Criminal Justice Services and the Ohio Association of Chiefs of Police for recognizing the issue of human trafficking and supporting this examination. Detective Ken Lawson of the Columbus Division of Police proved a valuable resource in too many ways to describe. We are grateful to all those who gave their time to share their experience with us and to the Toledo Public Library for facilitating our search of newspaper articles. We would like to thank Jay Albanese, Robert Davis, and Greg Ridgeway, who provided us comments on drafts, as well as Paul Steinberg and James Torr, who helped to fine-tune the resulting monograph.

Abbreviations

DOJ   U.S. Department of Justice

GAO   U.S. Government Accountability Office

ILO   International Labor Organization

IOM   International Organization for Migration

OVC   Office of Victims of Crime, U.S. Department of Justice

RICO   Racketeer Influenced and Corrupt Organizations Act

TVPA   Trafficking Victims Protection Act

UNODC   United Nations Office on Drugs and Crime

CHAPTER ONE

Introduction

Objective

This assessment explores the existence and characteristics of human trafficking—both sex and labor trafficking—in Ohio; its goals are to inform state and local policy aimed at preventing and responding to human trafficking and to guide practitioners who work with human-trafficking victims and who are responsible for responding to human-trafficking crimes.

Ohio has several characteristics that may be conducive to sex and labor trafficking. For example, it has several large urban centers, and much of the state's rural counties are producers of agriculture, both of which encompass significant immigrant and transient populations. Ohio is also close to the Canadian border and the eastern seaboard, so beyond being a destination state, it could serve as a transit point to other states. Although Ohio may host human-trafficking markets, little is known about trafficking in the state. Therefore, the Ohio Office of Criminal Justice Services and the Ohio Association of Chiefs of Police supported this analysis to provide Ohio-based policymakers and practitioners with information about their progress and needs in terms of responding to this type of crime.

In meeting these goals, we focus on three broad areas. First, we attempt to describe the minimum extent to which human trafficking occurs in Ohio (its existence) and its characteristics. We limit the analysis to concrete cases for which there is evidence supporting a trafficking offense. Our results, therefore, provide a conservative, lower-bound estimate of trafficking. We focus on describing the trafficking market in terms of the approximate number of people who have been victimized by trafficking in Ohio, the characteristics of such victims, and how victims come into contact with traffickers.

Second, we describe the awareness and response of the criminal justice community to human trafficking, focusing on answering such questions as how agencies become aware of human-trafficking cases and what factors facilitate or impede detection, investigation, and prosecution of human trafficking.

Finally, we explore how the social service community has responded to human trafficking, seeking to describe victims' critical needs so that policymakers and practitioners have a clearer understanding of how they may improve their assistance to trafficking victims.

In conducting the research here, we rely on the Trafficking Victims Protection Act (TVPA; contained in P.L. 106-386) definition of human trafficking:

> (A) sex trafficking in which a commercial sex act is induced by force, fraud, or coercion, or in which the person induced to perform such act has not attained 18 years of age; or

[handwritten margin note: forced or under-age prostitution]

> (B) the recruitment, harboring, transportation, provision, or obtaining of a person for labor or services, through the use of force, fraud, or coercion for the purpose of subjection to involuntary servitude, peonage, debt bondage, or slavery.

[handwritten margin note: forced labor]

This definition was chosen both because the study is interested in human trafficking in the United States and because many domestic studies use the TVPA definitions (e.g., Newman, 2006; Bales and Lize, 2005; Clawson et al., 2003).

It is important to clarify several aspects of the definition. First, there is a difference between human smuggling and human trafficking. Human smuggling is the facilitation, transportation, attempted transportation, or illegal entry of a person across an international border, in violation of one or more countries' laws, either clandestinely or through deception, such as the use of fraudulent documents (DOJ, 2006). Unlike smuggling, which is often a criminal, commercial transaction between two willing parties who go their separate ways once their business is complete, trafficking specifically targets the trafficked person as an object of criminal exploitation. The purpose from the beginning of the trafficking enterprise is to profit from the exploitation of the victim (DOS, 2006).

It is also important to note that human-trafficking victims need not be physically moved across any borders (city, state, or country) to be exploited for labor or commercial sex.

Finally, to be considered victims of sex trafficking, juveniles who particpate in commercial sex do not need to have been induced into it by fraud, force, or coercion. A juvenile is considered a sex-trafficking victim if he or she has any involvement whatsoever in commercial sex acts in which a third party benefits.

Background

The 1980s brought about an increased interest in human trafficking in the international arena, influenced by several factors, including immigration and migration patterns, the feminist movement, the AIDS crisis, and the publicity of child-sex tourism (Gozdziak and Collett, 2005). This interest led the UN General Assembly to adopt several provisions, including the Protocol to Prevent, Suppress, and Punish Trafficking in Persons, Especially Women and Children (UN, 2001).[1]

In the United States, media attention (along with other factors, such as work by the UN) partly fueled the increased federal attention paid to human trafficking, attention that has grown significantly in the past decade (Jahic and Finckenauer, 2005). Some argue that the widespread response to human trafficking by governments and nongovern-

---

[1] Through this protocol, the UN defines human trafficking as

[t]he recruitment, transportation, transfer, harbouring or receipt of persons, by means of the threat or use of force or other forms of coercion, of abduction, of fraud, of deception, of the abuse of power or of a position of vulnerability or of the giving or receiving of payments or benefits to achieve the consent of a person having control over another person, for the purpose of exploitation. Exploitation shall include, at a minimum, the exploitation of the prostitution of others or other forms of sexual exploitation, forced labour or services, slavery or practices similar to slavery, servitude or the removal of organs (p. 2).

mental organizations would not have occurred so rapidly without news stories about sympathetic victims who were presented more like the "girl next door" than previous images of women of color from Asia and Africa (Landesman, 2004; Jahic and Finckenauer, 2005).

In the United States, this growing interest culminated in the passage of the TVPA, which was signed into law in October 2000. This act and its subsequent 2003 and 2005 reauthorizations are the main tools used in combating both domestic and worldwide human trafficking (Gozdziak and Collett, 2005).

Beyond leading to legislation, the growing interest in human trafficking has also spurred an interest in research. Most of this research in the United States has been funded or conducted by the federal government.[2] For example, the federal government produces annual reports on the subject, such as the *Trafficking in Persons Report* (DOS, 2006), the *Attorney General's Annual Report to Congress on U.S. Government Activities to Combat Trafficking in Persons* (U.S. Attorney General's Office, 2006), and the Congressional Research Service's *Trafficking in Persons: The U.S. and International Response* (Miko, 2006), and monographs such as the CIA's *International Trafficking of Women to the United States: A Contemporary Manifestation of Slavery and Organized Crime* (Richard, 1999).

The National Institute of Justice (part of the Department of Justice [DOJ]) has been a leader in funding a diverse mix of external research and demonstration projects on human trafficking (Godziak and Collett, 2005). In addition, state-level work in Florida, Minnesota, and Washington has also sought to examine the cases, victims, and responses to the trafficking phenomenon.

Unfortunately, existing research has yet to move the field beyond estimating the scale of the problem; mapping routes and relationships among origin, transport, and destination countries; and reviewing the legal frameworks and policy responses to human trafficking (Godziak

---

[2] For useful listings of resources and research, see the Web pages on human trafficking maintained by the U.S. Departments of Health and Human Services (DHHS, undated), Homeland Security (DHS, 2006), Justice (DOJ, undated; National Institute of Justice, undated), Labor (DOL, undated), and State (DOS, undated).

and Collett, 2005). Such research is limited by a lack of consensus on the definition of *human trafficking* and by the operationalization of that definition, by the nature of the population itself, and by the difficulty of determining how to count human-trafficking victims.

Without a common definition, it is difficult to measure the phenomenon of human trafficking and provide comparable data on it. Some governments and academic researchers rely on the UN definition, some rely on the TVPA definition, and some develop their own definitions. Even if the same definition were applied and used, there would still be the problem of operationalizing the definition—that is, finding ways of distinguishing externally observable traits of trafficking victims. For example, if we observe fraud or coercion, and even involuntary servitude and debt bondage, it is still ambiguous whether we are observing human trafficking; determining whether human trafficking is taking place must rely on victims' or others' statements to this effect (Tyldum and Brunovskis, 2005).

Another fundamental challenge of conducting research on human trafficking is that the populations relevant to the study constitute so-called hidden populations, for which the size and boundaries are unknown and for whom no sampling frame exists (Tyldum and Brunovskis, 2005). Furthermore, because the behavior is illegal and stigmatized, participants may not want to cooperate with researchers. These factors significantly limit the availability of data to use as evidence in assessing human trafficking and formulating policy responses.

Agreement on how to count victims of human trafficking is also key to the quality of the research. To count the number of victims, we need to define what constitutes a victim and what does not. This has been done unevenly in existing research. Some countries and analysts continue to comingle data relating to trafficking, smuggling, and irregular migration (GAO, 2006). For example, some count all undocumented migrants assisted in crossing the border as being trafficked. Some view all transnational or migrant sex workers as trafficking victims, regardless of consent or conditions of labor. Some focus entirely on trafficking in women and girls for sexual exploitation, exclude men, and ignore labor trafficking. Others focus only on victims trafficked across international borders, ignoring domestic trafficking victims.

Given these problems, much of the existing research on trafficking attempts to show that it is a problem and to give a snapshot of that problem by relying on overviews, commentaries, and anecdotal information. Even more rigorous research tends to focus on the victims, especially certified victims or victims identified in the media, and less so on the traffickers, clients, and law enforcement agencies that may be involved (Andrees and van der Linden, 2005).

Approach

Given the nature of human trafficking and that the response to it may vary by local jurisdiction, this research examines two urban communities—Columbus and Toledo—to explore the characteristics of and response to human trafficking in Ohio. It is important to study more than one community so that potential variation can be identified. Yet given resource and time constraints, we had to choose a small sample of communities to study.

According to the Polaris Project, an international service and outreach organization with a mission to combat human trafficking, and other scholarly work, many factors make locations particularly susceptible to becoming destination or transit sites for human traffickers (Davis, 2006; Newman, 2006; Estes and Weiner, 2001). Many of these factors are found in Columbus and Toledo, including proximity to Canada (Toledo); extensive highway systems; growing immigrant populations; and proximity to large universities, international corporations, the agriculture industries (including dairy, nursery, and landscaping), and military bases. This same research further contends that economic (for example, the high poverty rate among minorities) and familial conditions (for example, high rates of child homelessness and teen pregnancy among some residents) may make Columbus and Toledo prime places for recruitment and kidnapping of sex-trafficking victims. In fact, a federal investigator, citing the high numbers of Toledo-area juvenile prostitutes and their traffickers surfacing in investigations outside Ohio, dubbed Toledo the "number one" teen prostitute–recruiting location in the United States (Erb and de Boer, 2006a).

Columbus is also the largest city in Ohio (and the 15th largest in the United States) and is the state capital, which make it a heavily visited city.

Given these factors and that the project team maintains extensive contacts with stakeholders in these two cities, Columbus and Toledo were chosen as case study sites. (See Appendix A for additional information on these cities relative to these characteristics.)

Analytical Techniques

Content Analysis. Human trafficking has increasingly gained the attention of federal and state governments. Given the focus on the issue and the seriousness of the crime, one would expect that human-trafficking arrests and their subsequent prosecutions would garner significant media attention (Raymond and Hughes, 2001; Albanese, Donnelly, and Kelegian, 2004; Dowling, Moreton, and Wright, 2007). This assumption underlies our newspaper content analysis, which attempts to identify and document actual trafficking incidents that occurred in the two study sites. As a basis for discussion, we focused on cases for which there was some form of evidence qualifying the incident as human trafficking under the TVPA definition. There is precedent for such an approach: Albanese, Donnelly, and Kelegian (2004) analyzed newspaper content to examine human trafficking in 18 U.S. cities for the 2002 calendar year.

We conducted an analysis of news articles spanning from January 1, 2003, to June 30, 2006, from the major newspaper in each case study site, the *Columbus Dispatch* and the *Toledo Blade*. We used 14 search terms to define content to be included in the analysis based on human-trafficking reports, analyses, and descriptions of trafficking cases: *brothel, immigrant, labor, massage, pimp, pornograph(y), prostitut(e), rape, sex, slave, sweatshop, traffic(king), underage,* and *undercover.*

To be as thorough as possible, we reviewed each abstract identified in the content analysis and included any article for full-text review that was potentially related to human trafficking. In addition, articles that made no mention of a case or an arrest were also included in the full-text review as potentially helpful as background material or leads toward additional cases.

Key Respondent Interviews. A critical component of this study was interacting with individuals working in the case study sites to understand their perspectives on the existence of human trafficking, its characteristics, and the criminal and juvenile justice and social service responses to the issue. We reviewed numerous human-trafficking surveys and interview instruments used in previous research and practice (including Raymond and Hughes, 2001; Minnesota Statistical Analysis Center, 2006; Wilson, Walsh, and Kleuber, 2006; and International Organization for Migration [IOM], 2005)[3] and developed our own instruments to solicit information about the existence of and local trends in human trafficking; case, victim, offender, and market characteristics; organizational responses to trafficking; collaboration; and recommendations for policy and practice. We also asked about specific cases identified in the newspaper content analysis.

We identified an initial list of possible key respondents through training and conference attendance registries, by organizational mission (local law enforcement, prosecutors, criminal and juvenile justice system personnel, immigration agencies, service providers, and advocacy agencies), and through recommendations from practitioners we knew to be involved in this issue. Using a snowball sampling technique, we then asked those we interviewed for suggestions about other key respondents knowledgeable about the issue who could provide additional information.

We requested interviews with 44 respondents representing 30 agencies. Ultimately, 26 respondents representing 19 agencies agreed to participate,[4] 11 of which represented the criminal justice system (five in Columbus and six in Toledo) and eight of which represented social

---

[3] IOM provided various instruments to the authors via email, December 13, 2005.

[4] The agencies included the Columbus Division of Police, Franklin County Sheriff, Federal Bureau of Investigation, Franklin County District Attorney's Office, Columbus City Attorney's Office, Toledo Police Department, Lucas County Sheriff, Lucas County Juvenile Probation, Lucas County Youth Treatment Center, Lucas County Juvenile Court, Lucas County District Attorney's Office, Ohio Behavioral Health Emergency Services, Community Refugee and Immigration Services, Maryhaven (an addiction recovery facility), Sexual Assault Resource Network of Central Ohio, Wake Up Youth, Farm Labor Organizing Committee, Second Chance, and Lucas County Job and Family Services.

service providers (four in Columbus and four in Toledo).[5] The criminal justice agencies included local and federal law enforcement and prosecutors, probation officers, judges, and secure placement directors. The social service providers included health providers, sexual assault recovery service providers, prostitution recovery service providers, immigrant service providers, and behavioral health and human service agencies. The interviews took place from February through July 2007.

Study Limitations

As with any analysis, it is important to understand its limitations. One concern with analyses of this type is selection bias, which may occur in four forms. First, it is possible (and highly probable) that the articles we discovered in the newspaper content analysis do not reflect all cases of human trafficking that are known or that occurred. It is therefore possible that the cases not reported in the newspapers are different from those that are reported in the newspapers, thereby limiting the extent to which the characteristics of the cases we assessed from that source can be generalized to all cases. This also means our assessment of the existence of human trafficking must be interpreted as a minimum baseline or lower-bound estimate.

Second and similarly, we attempted to interview those likely to be most knowledgeable about human trafficking. Their assessments and perspectives may be different from those who declined to participate or those who may have not been included on our contact list, including victims. This limits the extent to which we can generalize their responses to similar stakeholders.

Third, it is possible that respondents may over- or understate the problem, depending on their recollection and the extent to which they want to draw attention to the issue. Our focus on concrete cases helps

---

[5] The relatively low response rate results partly from starting with a large registry of human-trafficking training participants, many of whom, when contacted, were interested in the issue but were not knowledgeable about it.

to limit overstatements, but we have no way of determining whether the problem was understated for some reason.

Finally, we examined two nonrandom cities in Ohio. They may not be representative of the entire human-trafficking experience in Ohio. Readers should bear these limitations in mind while interpreting the findings and consider the results as based on known, but not necessarily representative, examples.

Outline of This Monograph

The following three chapters rely on the content analysis and key respondent interviews conducted in the case study sites of Columbus and Toledo to describe the human-trafficking market (Chapter Two) and the justice and service community responses to the problem (Chapters Three and Four, respectively). They are based on "concrete cases"—those with evidence suggesting that they qualify as human trafficking based on the TVPA definition. The final chapter provides policy considerations based on the overall analysis.

Appendix A provides background information on Columbus and Toledo. Appendix B contains the references for the content analysis. Appendix C contains short summaries of the concrete cases identified as part of the analysis, while Appendix D contains a discussion of some of the constructive cases—cases suggestive of human trafficking but not definitive enough to be classified as concrete cases.

CHAPTER TWO

The Human-Trafficking Markets in Columbus and Toledo

One of the key goals of this research was to characterize the human-trafficking markets in Columbus and Toledo, Ohio. This chapter uses the results of the content analysis and interviews to do that. First, we discuss the existence and estimates of human trafficking in Ohio. Then, we describe some of the characteristics of the human-trafficking market. Whenever relevant, we present our analysis within the larger context of the literature on human trafficking. Finally, at the end of the chapter, we compare the two case study sites.

Existence of Human Trafficking

A wide range of estimates exists on the scope and magnitude of human trafficking, both internal and transnational. The International Labor Organization (ILO)—the UN agency charged with addressing labor standards, employment, and social protection issues—estimates that there are 12.3 million people in forced labor, bonded labor, forced child labor, and sexual servitude at any given time; other estimates range from 4 million to 27 million (DOS, 2006). The U.S. Department of State produced estimates of the annual worldwide trafficked population at 800,000 to 900,000, with 14,500 to 17,500 trafficked into the United States alone.

These estimates, while widely quoted, are questioned by many, including the U.S. Government Accountability Office (GAO), which reviewed the estimation methods used by the U.S. government, ILO, the United Nations Office on Drugs and Crime (UNODC), and IOM. GAO (2006) found that all of these estimates are questionable because of methodological weaknesses, gaps in data, and numerical discrepancies. Limitations include inability to replicate estimates, estimates based on unreliable estimates of others, estimates lacking internal trafficking data, and estimates not suitable for analysis over time. It goes on to report that country data are generally not available, reliable, or comparable and that there is considerable discrepancy between the numbers of observed and estimated victims of human trafficking.

The only verifiable U.S. data document the number of trafficking victims officially certified by the Department of Health and Human Services, Office of Refugee Resettlement. From 2001 to 2005, the office issued 841 certifications or letters of eligibility to receive federally funded benefits as trafficking victims (DOJ, 2006). Clearly, there is a huge discrepancy between the number of certified victims per year— 230 in 2005—and the estimated 14,500 to 17,500 victims trafficked into the United States each year. This raises questions about whether the estimates are extremely exaggerated or whether trafficking victims are almost never discovered, or at least rarely processed as trafficking victims by the federal government. Given measurement difficulties, more recent attempts to assess the number of victims have begun developing statistical models to produce estimates based on source and transit assumptions (Clawson, Layne, and Small, 2006).

Our own analysis provides a minimum baseline or lower-bound estimate of human trafficking in our case study sites based on the content analysis and interviews discussed in Chapter One. Table 2.1 summarizes the results of the analysis. In total, there were nearly 18,000 articles uncovered using the 14 search terms listed in Chapter One, with the *Columbus Dispatch* yielding about 3,000 more articles than the *Toledo Blade*. From these, we selected 585 articles for full-text review, which included a second and complete review of the article. Of those, we determined 64 articles to be relevant to human trafficking. These are referenced in Appendix B.

Of the relevant articles, 28 highlighted four concrete cases of human trafficking, all of which involved juveniles engaged in com-

Table 2.1
Content Analysis and Respondent Summary Results, Concrete Cases

Source	Columbus	Toledo	Total/ Average
Content analysis			
Number of articles identified by search terms	10,428	7,420	17,848
Full-text reviews	310	275	585
Articles relevant to human trafficking	23	41	64
Articles referencing concrete trafficking cases	0	28	28
Total concrete cases identified from content analysis	0	4	4
Percentage of key respondents referencing concrete trafficking cases	42[a]	71[b]	58
Total additional concrete cases identified from key respondent interviews	5	6	11
Total concrete cases from both sources	5	10	15

[a] n = 5.
[b] n = 10.

mercial sex and all of which were in Toledo. Seventeen articles revealed seven cases for which there was not sufficient information in the articles to verify the existence of human trafficking. In the interviews, we probed these incidents, which included prosecutions of brothels fronting as legitimate businesses as well as potential instances of forced labor.

As shown in the second-to-last row of Table 2.1, the interviews yielded discussion of 11 additional concrete cases of human trafficking. Further, 58 percent (n = 15) of respondents, 42 percent (n = 5) in Columbus and 71 percent (n = 10) in Toledo, indicated that they were aware of cases of human trafficking. Not all of these refer to the cases we count as concrete. For example, a criminal justice respondent in Columbus recalled the existence of juveniles arrested for prostitution who would qualify as trafficked victims. Similarly, a respondent from a prostitution recovery program in Toledo recalled the existence of sex-trafficking victims. However, they could not provide enough information to allow us to characterize individual cases. Therefore, Table 2.1 does not count this information in any of the rows that calculate total concrete cases, but it does include the references to this information in the row showing the percentage of key respondents referencing cases. All told, the analysis yielded 15 concrete cases of human trafficking, five in Columbus and 10 in Toledo, as shown in the bottom, shaded row in Table 2.1. Appendix C describes the concrete cases, which are numbered 1–15 for reference purposes.

About one-quarter (n = 6) of respondents also identified incidents or cases with possible ties to human trafficking. Some of the respondents felt that additional cases or incidents contained the elements of human trafficking. However, they could not articulate evidence necessary to qualify them under the TVPA definition of human trafficking that we used in this study. This does not mean that trafficking did not occur in these cases, just that there was not sufficient information to support it. These case types are worth noting because respondents contend that they may be associated with human trafficking, they may turn out to be human trafficking if investigated as such, and they may provide important training and policy lessons. We do not base our analyses on these cases, because they are not concrete cases. Rather, we summarize them in Appendix D as additional background information.

We identified two types of concrete cases of human trafficking. The first type involves commercial sex trafficking of children. These cases have a similar fact pattern, with all involving Toledo-area juveniles lured or abducted into commercial sex trafficking by one or more adult offenders who benefit from the transactions. This type of case was identified in both the content analysis (by the 28 articles in the *Toledo Blade*) and by respondents in Toledo. The second type of concrete case was not discovered in the content analysis but instead through key respondent interviews in Columbus. These cases involve the exploitation and forced labor of either foreign nationals or of spouses.

The content analysis and interviews with key respondents revealed evidence supporting the existence of human-trafficking cases in both Columbus and Toledo, as discussed earlier and shown in the bottom row of Table 2.1. Taken together and categorized by type, the analysis identified five labor-trafficking cases in Columbus (four domestic servitude[1] and one hotel exploitation) and 10 cases of sex trafficking being investigated/prosecuted involving Toledo-area actors (all commercial sex involving juveniles, with some of the ongoing investigations also including adults). At the time of the study, law enforcement agencies in Toledo were investigating 60 possible human traffickers as part of six of these cases.

At the time of the study, four of the five Columbus-area cases were unknown to law enforcement, while six of the 10 Toledo-area cases were being investigated by law enforcement, and four of these cases were in the prosecution stage or had been adjudicated. Where information is known, the number of victims in each case ranges from one to at least 10.

In addition to actual cases, estimates of the number of human-trafficking victims *seen* in a given year range from one respondent's estimate of two or three per year to another respondent's estimate of 50 to 75 per year. The majority of respondents (n = 7) and evidence from cases discussed in the content analysis suggest something in between these two estimates—somewhere between 12 and 20 victims per year.

Although there is a small number of identified cases relative to other crimes, this is also true nationally. The federal government filed just 124 cases between 2001 and 2006, and only 238 defendants had been convicted under TVPA as of December 2006 (DOJ, 2007). The problem may also still be emerging. At the time of the study, Toledo's task force had been in place less than one year, and law enforcement officials there suggest that these cases take a long time to investigate and bring to trial. Further, most respondents believe that the problem is significantly larger than they know. Two Toledo-area service providers and one Lucas County Juvenile Court judge suggested that there

---

[1]   Cases of domestic servitude have appeared elsewhere in the United States. A recent survey of victim service providers in Minnesota revealed that half of the respondents who indicated working with human-trafficking victims reported working with individuals exploited in domestic servitude situations (Minnesota Statistical Analysis Center, 2006). Similarly, three of 12 human-trafficking cases identified and examined by Bales and Lize (2005) in southwest Florida; Washington, D.C.; and Chicago involved domestic service in U.S. homes.

are as many as three to 10 trafficking victims of this type for every one identified.

It is not entirely clear whether the size of the problem has changed in recent years. One respondent suggested that, as recently as the 1980s, child prostitution was against all norms within prostitution rings, whereas today it is the norm. However, many respondents felt that the issue has always existed, but that there is increased awareness of it today. Without firm data, it is not possible to characterize whether or how this problem has changed.

Characteristics of Human Trafficking: Victims and Traffickers

Beyond determining estimates of how much human trafficking is occurring in the Columbus and Toledo case study sites, we also wanted to better understand the characteristics of human trafficking in the two areas as revealed in our content analysis and interviews. Here, we discuss both the victims and the traffickers in terms of several dimensions.

Victim Characteristics

Juvenile victims of sex trafficking in our case studies are almost exclusively female, ranging in age from 10 to 17, and are equally likely to be black as white. There is also a small percentage of Hispanic victims in each study site. Almost all were thought to be born and raised in the United States, most typically in the local (Columbus or Toledo) area. This is in contrast to Albanese, Donnelly, and Kelegian's (2004) finding that the vast majority of reported victims is from other areas of the world, most notably Mexico, Central America, Asia, or Russia. Very little information is known about victims in our labor-trafficking cases, but what is known suggests that the victims are primarily women born outside the United States in countries such as Russia, Ethiopia, Eritrea, Guinea, and Morocco.

Recruitment of Victims

There is considerable agreement in the literature that victims of human trafficking are more often lured or recruited into trafficking than abducted (Newman, 2006). This view is supported by respondents (n = 8) in Toledo, who suggest that juvenile sex-trafficking victims are often runaways or are on the street because of family or substance abuse problems.

Cases 4 and 1 illustrate this point. In case 4, the offender befriended a 15-year-old who ran away from foster care and was living on the streets. He offered the girl food, housing, and drugs, and eventually exploited her as a prostitute.

In case 1, a South Toledo teen, whose mother was a prostitute and addicted to drugs and alcohol, had been molested for years by family friends. She started rebelling against a mother who she felt should have recognized the abuse, and she thought life with a pimp sounded fascinating. She called a pimp she heard about from a friend and asked whether she could join him in Harrisburg. He asked her whether she knew what she was getting herself into, and she said she did.

According to both local law enforcement respondents (n = 3) and social service providers (n = 2), there are also girls who seek prostitution for what they perceive to be its glamorous lifestyle or are recruited by pimps who are thought to solicit in area shopping malls. The potential attraction of the lifestyle is hinted at by case 1, in which a Toledo-area youth was presumably drawn to the perceived glamor of prostitution. She was 16 and "hanging out" at a bus stop when a man she hardly knew pulled up to her. She got in because she liked his car, and he drove her to Detroit, where she began a life of prostitution.

However, in at least two of the Toledo-area cases (cases 3 and 2), the victims were actually abducted by their traffickers. In case 3. two cousins—ages 14 and 15—were on their way to get a milkshake when a couple lured them into their car, took them out to eat, and then back to a Toledo house where an alarm system was set and they were not permitted to leave. Once in the house, a 40-year-old man and two women, ages 24 and 19, separated the cousins and "indoctrinated" them. The cousins were told "how to behave [and] solicit customers."

In case 2, the victim went out with her 19-year-old boyfriend for her 14th birthday. She thought they were going to the movies; instead, they spent several days moving among various homes in Toledo and Michigan. This is where they met the boyfriend's relatives and friends, including a man and woman who soon became her captors. The male, a one-time Toledo resident, promised to take the girl home but instead took her to Indiana and Pennsylvania where he beat and twice raped her and forced her to prostitute herself at various truck stops.

As Estes and Weiner (2001) found in their study of human trafficking, there were also reports of parents or other family members prostituting their children or, in one case, trading their grandchild for crack. These cases are thought to be rarer.

Very little is known about recruitment tactics used on the domestic servitude and hotel labor-trafficking victims in Columbus. However, what is known suggests that victims were promised opportunities by well-respected individuals with high profiles in their communities.

Victim-Trafficker Relationships

The relationships between the victims of sex trafficking and their traffickers can be complicated. Estes and Weiner (2001) report evidence that some women had intimate relationships with the men who pimped them. Typically, a pimp befriends a homeless girl, spends lavish sums of money on her, and pays attention to her. Sex between them is taken for granted. In time, the pimp convinces her to have sex for money, all of which is turned over to him. The relationship gradually becomes less emotional and more contractual, with financial quotas set for each night. Not infrequently, the pimp will father a child with the girl to deepen his control over her.

Case 1 of our analysis exhibits this type of relationship. In that case, according to federal authorities, "Snow" was beaten by the man who is now serving a 40-year sentence for his role in the trafficking ring, yet she is reportedly upset that her pimp is going to face so much time and still finds him "sexy." Looking back, she claims not to have enjoyed the work, but she enjoyed the money and the perks. Her pimp took her and others to Universal Studios and bought her clothes and jewelry. However, she did not return home with anything of value.

In some cases, it is the prostitute who recruits her pimp.

For the labor-trafficking cases, little is known about the relationships between victim and trafficker, except to reiterate that the trafficker is typically well respected in the community, so there is some indication that being chosen by the trafficker to come to the United States is something that may be initially sought after, not avoided. This finding is echoed in a study of human trafficking in Minnesota, which describes the case of a Nigerian woman who was brought to the United States by a distant relative—a prominent doctor—and forced to work without pay (Minnesota Statistical Analysis Center, 2006). This situation has also been seen with diplomats who bring individuals to the United States to work as nannies or housecleaners. There have been many accusations of exploitation, but diplomatic immunity provides an additional barrier to prosecution (Taylor, 2007).

Working Locations and Conditions

The sex-trafficking rings seem to operate similarly. In three of the four cases for which details are known and in cases still under investigation, the victims were transported across state lines—to places such as Ohio, Michigan, Indiana, Illinois, Arkansas, Virginia, Georgia, Maryland, Tennessee, Pennsylvania, California, Florida, Louisiana, and the District of Columbia—where teens were rotated among motels, truck stops, and highway welcome centers. In one case, the victims were also prostituted in Toledo-area hotels at least a dozen times. Law enforcement respondents suggested that the girls are also moved to take advantage of opportunities—such as conventions, sporting events, or one-time appearances in "cathouses."

The literature supports the market for girls in areas inhabited by large numbers of transient males. Estes and Weiner (2001) describe five types of transient males who may make up a considerable customer base for trafficked children: military personnel, truck drivers, seasonal workers, conventioneers, and sex tourists. At least two of these markets were mentioned in our study—the markets for girls at truck stops and the market for girls near conventions and sporting events.

There is little information in our case studies about the profits from trafficking, but what we know suggests that they can be considerable. One truck stop in Pennsylvania where Toledo-area girls were trafficked was often "jammed" with truckers by late afternoon, especially "party row," where much of the prostitution took place. There was so much demand that an individual prostitute could make more than $1,000 per night. In another case, the victim made more than $300 on her first night. Furthermore, prosecution and asset forfeiture records suggest that those involved in one ring are accused of wiring at least $310,000 in proceeds to one another and risk losing up to $1 million in asset forfeiture if convicted of their crimes.

On a macro scale, there can be huge profits from women trafficked for sex work, with estimates suggesting profits as high as $7 billion to $10 billion per year (Cwikel and Hoban, 2005, p. 306; Clawson et al., 2003). On a micro scale, estimates prepared by the Polaris Project suggest that one trafficker made approximately $632,000 in one year from prostituting four young women and girls (Davis, 2006). International criminals appear to be increasingly shifting from drug trafficking to human trafficking because profits are higher, humans are easier to move and store, and there are fewer risks (Clawson et al., 2003).

In the labor (domestic servitude and hotel exploitation) cases, the situation is similar. Individuals are forced to work long hours with little or no pay. Further, in cases in the literature and in cases identified in our case study sites, domestic servitude among women often includes violence and rape.

Physical and Psychological Control and Abuse

The principal methods traffickers use to control their victims include taking away their travel and identity documents, threatening to turn them in to local police, sexual abuse, threats of and actual physical violence, isolation, and debt bondage (Bales and Lize, 2005; Schauer and Wheaton, 2006). We found that most of these tactics were used by traffickers and their associates in the cases we identified.

In our labor-trafficking cases, some victims' documents were taken and the victims were threatened with deportation or jail. In all cases, their freedom of movement was severely curtailed, and, in some cases, they were beaten and raped.

Similar tactics were used on the juvenile sex-trafficking victims identified in our case study sites. Victims were often given new identities and were taught to never give their real name or age to the police. Some were forced to memorize their identities by writing all their fake information repeatedly on paper. Law enforcement officials call this "the name game" and admit that, if they have the interest and the personnel, they spend hours, and even days, trying to determine the correct identity of victims.

There was widespread physical and psychological abuse reported. The abuse is perpetrated by the traffickers, by other victims who acted as enforcers, and by customers. This is exemplified in case 2, in which a 14-year-old girl abducted on her birthday was repeatedly raped and beaten by her captors and two other victims were also reportedly beaten if they did not follow the rules. One victim reveals that it was not the transactional sex that surprised her—it was the violence, and, although she thought her pimp was pretty good to her, she knew of others who did not make it out alive.

On the issue of brutality, law enforcement respondents contended that they have seen everything from pistol whipping to broken bones. At least four of the Toledo men connected with one of the cases had been previously accused of violence, including rape, beatings with a chain, and bottle smashing.

Two victims connected to case 1 have been murdered since the case began. One girl ran away from home when she was 11, was raped when she was 13, and was in and out of mental health treatment, child welfare, and court services. She was addicted to drugs, traded sex for drugs at an early age, and eventually became part of the sex-trafficking ring. Her overdose death meant the loss of a witness for the prosecution. Another woman, who was at one time married to one of the Toledo pimps indicted in one of the cases, was brutally murdered. Police believe she was killed by one of several long-haul truckers who are also serial killers. She was found at the back of the 10-acre truck stop near Indianapolis.

A Pennsylvania state trooper suggested that it was violence associated with prostitution in Pennsylvania that led to the investigations and prosecution of one of the major sex-trafficking rings connected to the Toledo area (Erb and de Boer, 2006b).

However, the pimps' stories differed. One offender considered himself a "player," not a pimp. The distinction has to do with how he handled the prostitutes. He said that he was not aggressive, yet he had been accused by law enforcement at least three times of breaking women's noses. He insisted, however, that he did not have to force women—that they "love the game." Other defendants agreed, suggesting that, if the girls were scared or being forced, they could have sought help from the police.

There is no consensus about whether victims in our case studies had freedom of movement or not. Two respondents felt that, in some instances, girls were free to leave if they could. Three other respondents felt that they are highly supervised and not permitted free movement. There was evidence of both explanations in the content analysis. Explanations also varied about why victims do not seek help; these include stigma, the perceived judgmental attitude of service providers, drug addiction, and having nowhere to turn. This echoes Estes and Weiner's (2001) finding that women who ultimately leave the sex industry often report that economic necessity, drug dependencies, and threats from traffickers originally prevented their departure.

Characteristics of Traffickers and Their Associates

The offenders in our case studies also show similarities. In the labor-trafficking cases, as discussed above, most of the traffickers were prominent doctors or businesspeople, with money, influence, and respect in their communities. The service provider who worked with the victims in these cases felt that these traffickers acted alone, without coconspirators.

The number of offenders involved in the juvenile sex-trafficking cases ranged from one to at least 14, and many of the known cases involved both men and women. The ages of offenders ranged from 22 to 43 for the men and 19 to 27 for the women. All have residence in or residency ties to Toledo, where all the cases for which we have trafficker information originated. For example, in one case, the traffickers included a 40-year-old man and two women ages 24 and 19. In another case, at least 12 men and two women were among those Toledo residents listed as defendants. Their ages ranged from 23 to 27 for the women and from 22 to 43 for the men. Similar to the characteristics of pimps reported by Estes and Weiner (2001), the majority of pimps in our case study sites are reported to be black and they reportedly control anywhere from one to seven girls at a time.

Respondents explained that women were key in indoctrinating and training the victims on "how to behave [and] solicit customers." The women, even the victims themselves, also play important roles in recruiting other women and enforcing the rules of the traffickers. The roles of women in trafficking rings documented in the literature suggest a similar picture (e.g., Davis, 2006).

Information about the traffickers in our case study sites is limited; however, one article profiles a sex trafficker, who was convicted and sentenced to 40 years in a federal penitentiary (de Boer and Erb, 2006b). The trafficker was proud of his lineage as a third-generation pimp:

> He was raised in the lifestyle and learned it at a young age, traveling with his father across the country and considering himself an up and coming player. He had reportedly done everything— including running a multi-state car theft ring, but actually pimped by his 16th birthday when he was recruited by a girl who wanted to work for him. He claims to be a gentleman and asserts that there is a code to pimping. Some of his workers agree and suggest that he bought them clothes, gave them money, and took them to amusement parks. Despite this, he is also accused by law enforcement of using violence to lure prostitutes across state lines and force them into sex (de Boer and Erb, 2006b, p. A1).

In at least one known case, the crime was not the first sex offense committed by the trafficker. In this case, the trafficker had been convicted 10 prior times for sex-related crimes. In 1997, the offender allegedly ran an escort service from his home in North Toledo, with as many as 20 prostitutes, including a 15-year-old girl.

Law enforcement respondents suggested that traffickers also deal drugs and are involved in other crimes. Four criminal justice respondents indicated that recruiting or prostituting girls is sometimes linked to gang activity. This finding is supported in other domestic studies of human trafficking, which have reported that human traffickers are engaged in a wide range of crimes both against their victims (rape, assault, extortion, homicide, abductions) and against the state (money laundering, tax evasion, document fraud, and corruption of officials) (Bales and Lize, 2005).

The literature suggests that there are a number of potential players in a human-trafficking organization, including organizers, middlemen, business operators, and corrupt government officials and police who are paid to look the other way (Schauer and Wheaton, 2006). There is little information in the cases we discovered about the associates or coconspirators of traffickers. However, three local law enforcement respondents suggested that the people involved know only what they need to know to do their jobs. They do not know the traffickers' names, or at least their real names, and whole operations can be run from the homes of traffickers without them ever coming in contact with the victims themselves.

In addition, our analysis reveals that individuals other than the traffickers were charged in connection to one of the trafficking cases. Two stepbrothers of one of the defendants were charged with traveling to the defendant's home and destroying photographs of pimps and women involved in the investigation. They were charged with obstruction of justice, destruction of evidence, and conspiracy and face up to 25 years in prison and $500,000 in fines.

Another defendant fled and, with FBI agents trailing him, hid in the crawl space of a Toledo-area home. Three women, ages 19, 20, and 21, living in the home hid the man and lied to federal agents executing a search. Agents found him and the three women, two of whom had been arrested previously on prostitution charges in the Harrisburg, Pennsylvania, area, were charged in federal court for conspiring to hide the suspect from the agents.

Organization of Trafficking and Its Relation to Organized Crime

There is debate among law enforcement officials and others about the level of organization of sex-trafficking rings. Federal indictments suggest that there is a high level of organization among pimps who manage the business: setting prices, establishing work schedules, and negotiating turf. One prosecutor described a sex-trafficking ring as a "loose confederacy" of pimps, each with his own turf but enough reason to get along. They even sometimes traded and sold prostitutes back and forth.

Others, including four criminal justice respondents in Toledo, felt that trafficking rings are less organized than local gangs or drug-selling organizations. All (in Toledo) agreed that the victims are moved from place to place, but there were differences of opinion about the level of coordination. Some thought pimps would not lend or give up control of their victims and that they move them to other cities to take advantage of opportunities, such as conferences or other events. Others thought that they were passed off through a network of offenders.

There is also disagreement in the literature. Although early U.S. government statements claimed that sex trafficking was largely controlled by organized crime, it is now believed that individual entrepreneurs and small, organized groups are the perpetrators of most of the trafficking in the United States (Schauer and Wheaton, 2006). Moreover, Finckenauer and Liu (2006) asserted that the role of organized crime groups in human trafficking has been exaggerated—that there is little hard evidence of organized crime involvement in the trafficking of persons. Despite this, two studies of U.S. local law enforcement suggest that local law enforcement officials perceive human trafficking to be perpetrated by organized crime (Wilson, Walsh, and Kleuber, 2006; Estes and Weiner, 2001). One survey found that local law enforcement officials perceive human trafficking to be perpetrated by transnational organized crime networks (75 percent agree) or large, national organized crime networks (64 percent agree) over local organized crime networks (41 percent agree) or individuals without organized crime connections (39 percent agree) (Wilson, Walsh, and Kleuber, 2006).

In all but one of the labor-trafficking cases, organized crime does not appear to be involved. It is possible, however, that the case involving the exploitation of Russian victims in the hotel industry may involve a more formally organized structure with possible ties to other businesses. We could not confirm this.

Columbus and Toledo Comparison

The juvenile sex-trafficking markets, to the extent that they could be identified, were similar in Toledo and Columbus. However, there were many more articles and respondents who could describe this market in Toledo than there were in Columbus. Nearly all aspects of our analysis in Columbus suggest that there is not a significant juvenile sex-trafficking market there. While one of the respondents could recall the existence of child victims of sex trafficking (even though he did not initially recognize them to be human-trafficking victims), none of the respondents could identify a specific trafficking case in the area or a case that involved area victims or offenders. Despite sparse information, one reported difference in these two markets is the extent of interstate movement of victims in Columbus, where there was thought to be very little or no movement of juveniles across government boundaries to participate in commercial sex acts.

In contrast to our analysis of Columbus, our analysis of Toledo suggests that this city may play a significant regional or national role in the sex trafficking of juveniles. Individuals associated with the cases identified through the newspaper content analysis suggested that Toledo is an integral part of the sex-trafficking business, supplying the top management (the pimps), the middle management (adult prostitutes who train and discipline the other prostitutes), and the product (young girls lured, kidnapped, or sold into the business).[2] Although Toledo-area respondents indicated that they do not know why Toledo would

---

[2]   A federal investigator told a Lucas County Juvenile Court official that Toledo was the "number one" teen prostitute–recruiting location in the United States (Erb and de Boer, 2006a). Our analysis uncovered only a few examples of pimps recruiting teens and then transporting them out of the city to engage in prostitution. It is possible that this occurs with greater frequency than we could determine because the recruitment is not detected in Toledo. However, without this information and information about what is occuring in other U.S. communities, our analysis can neither confirm nor deny this claim.

play this prominent a role in the sex trafficking of minors, they did offer a number of the conditions described in the literature as indicative of sex trafficking. These factors include high negative social indicators for children, including homelessness, physical and sexual abuse and neglect, substance abuse, teen pregnancy, poverty, and gang involvement, as well as the existence of adult prostitution markets.

In the case of labor trafficking, no market was found in Toledo. The market in Columbus was identified by four respondents (representing two agencies). Given this, there is no basis of comparison between the two sites.

CHAPTER THREE

Justice System Response

Beyond identifying cases of human trafficking in the two case study sites, we wanted to understand how the justice system in those two sites responds to cases of human trafficking. This chapter discusses that response, focusing on such questions as how agencies become aware of human-trafficking cases and what factors facilitate or impede detection, investigation, and prosecution of human trafficking. Our analysis is based primarily on interviews with individuals in the justice system in the two case study sites, as well as on information from the content analysis.

Here, we examine the response, beginning first with a discussion of training and resources and then moving on to discussions about identifying victims, treating victims, investigating and prosecuting cases, charges and penalties for such cases, and the role of criminal statutes in such cases. We conclude, as we did in the previous chapter, with a comparison between the two case study sites.

Training and Resources

Select staff in nearly all the law enforcement organizations (10 of 11) that participated in our study received training on human trafficking. In Columbus, most of the training was provided by local experts or the state; in Toledo, this training was provided by local experts and by the federal government. Respondents received markedly more training than average: A survey conducted in 2006 of local law enforcement agencies found that only seven agencies (8 percent of their sample) reported having conducted or received training in human trafficking (Wilson, Walsh, and Kleuber, 2006).

According to the same survey, only four of the departments indicated that they had personnel assigned to deal exclusively with issues involving human trafficking, although 37 percent acknowledged that the department had personnel or a unit whose duties would include addressing human-trafficking issues or cases. Various divisions of vice, organized crime, crimes against persons, child exploitation, and detective bureaus were most frequently listed as the units responsible for addressing human-trafficking issues (Wilson, Walsh, and Kleuber, 2006). In our case study sites, the situation was mixed. In Toledo, the two main local law enforcement agencies had staff dedicated to human-trafficking cases; those personnel were assigned to a federal task force. In Columbus, there were no dedicated staff, and the issue might be handled under several different units, including the special investigations unit in the sheriff's department and either or both the special victims or sexual assault unit or the narcotics or vice units in the Columbus Division of Police.

None of the local, state, or federal law enforcement agencies that participated in our study in Columbus have dedicated human-trafficking resources, but resources do exist in Toledo. The federally funded task force provides support for personnel, overtime, equipment, and computer forensic support.

Identification of Victims

Numerous studies point out that local police officers are likely to first encounter victims and perpetrators of human trafficking (Wilson, Walsh, and Kleuber, 2006; de Baca and Tisi, 2002; Finckenauer and Lui, 2006; Newman, 2006). Traffic accidents, tips, and border checks are additional ways in which victims are identified by law enforcement (Albanese, Donnelly, and Kelegian, 2004). Further, in a study of human trafficking in southwest Florida; Washington, D.C.; and Chicago, Bales and Lize (2005) find that trafficking victims often have contact with local law enforcement authorities, but in 11 of the 12 cases they examined, these authorities failed to notice the victims and take appropriate action to bring them to safety. In this study, the victims in one-third (n = 4) of the cases secured their own freedom by escaping their exploiters; in another one-third (n = 4) of cases, a private citizen took an interest and helped liberate the victims. In just one case did law enforcement agencies identify the victim.

The methods of identification and rescue in our case study sites are similar to those reported by Bales and Lize (2005). We have specific information about victim identification in all five of the labor-trafficking cases. In each of these cases, the victim was identified by service providers; law enforcement was notified in only one case.

In the four juvenile sex-trafficking cases for which information about victim identification is known, one victim was identified by a service provider when she developed a sexually transmitted disease, was hospitalized, and then transferred to a drug rehabilitation center, where she told authorities about her experiences. Another victim escaped with the help of a private citizen, a female trucker who let her enter her cab and transported her to safety. In another case, the victim told her trafficker that she was done with prostituting. He beat her, and when law enforcement authorities arrested her later that day, she told police her story. Finally, in one case, local law enforcement officers in another state first arrested the victim and then identified her as a trafficking victim. In this case, which was case 3 in our analysis, the victim was caught with a trucker near Ann Arbor, Michigan. Though the sheriff's deputies could not prove prostitution, they reportedly had a gut feeling that the young girl's story was not true. Once she was alone with the officers, she told the truth. They called the FBI and the victim's family.

More generally, the way that juvenile sex-trafficking victims are identified in Toledo has changed markedly in recent years. Today, victims come to the task force's attention through vice officers, street officers, and juvenile court officials, such as judges, probation officers, and placement directors, as well as through social service providers, who refer them. Before recent cases brought the human-trafficking issue to the forefront in Toledo, officials reportedly had little idea that these girls were involved in trafficking, and they were not identified as victims.

This is still the case in Columbus, where juveniles who participate in organized sex rings run by adults are not identified as trafficking victims. They are arrested for prostitution or related crimes and are processed by the juvenile justice system without examination of the possible deeper issues, including human trafficking.

Treatment of Potential Victims

Our interviews indicate that the response of the Toledo justice system to the issue of trafficking of juveniles has also changed markedly in recent years; justice system actors suggest that, in the past, the system did not realize that there was a problem until knowledge of the problem was thrust upon them as a result of the initiation of two large federal child sex-trafficking cases involving Toledo-area actors. In response to these cases, the system, especially the juvenile justice system, has moved toward attempting to identify trafficking victims and treating them as such.

Federal and local law enforcement and juvenile justice personnel indicated that they systematically debrief prostitutes, especially juvenile prostitutes, for connections to human trafficking. They are still arrested, but they are treated more as victims than as offenders. Frequently, according to law enforcement, they are willing to tell their stories, at least as much as they know (which often is not much), about their traffickers. Whatever law enforcement agencies learn is kept in a database, which is maintained by the FBI and used to build cases. Numerous victims have cooperated with law enforcement and testified at grand jury and trial proceedings.

In contrast, the juvenile justice system in Columbus treats juveniles arrested for prostitution as offenders instead of victims. Employing prosecution as the primary response mechanism, prosecutors may seek to have them held in lock-up so that they can be assessed, but usually the juveniles are officially processed and released. According to respondents, these cases are not treated as possible human-trafficking cases and are not investigated or prosecuted as such by federal law enforcement.

In addition, according to respondents in both Toledo and Columbus, the child welfare systems cannot or do not do much to identify or assist these youth victims. These factors effectively inhibit the identification and provision of services that these juveniles need and undermine efforts to obtain information about the other offenders (and potentially other victims) involved in the trafficking process.

Toledo-area respondents explained that they are working to design and implement formal protocols to identify, assess, and treat possible trafficking victims, although they do not currently exist. This is the case in Columbus, with the majority of law enforcement agencies (98 percent) reporting having no policies or protocols in place to deal with trafficking victims (Wilson, Walsh, and Kleuber, 2006).

Investigating and Prosecuting Cases

To investigate and prosecute domestic sex-trafficking cases as defined in the TVPA, law enforcement tactics must change from a single agency processing and releasing prostitutes to "following the money." This change has reportedly not been made in Columbus but has begun to be made in Toledo and by the agencies that participated in cases that involve Toledo-area actors.

[handwritten annotation: following the money]

This transition is seen most clearly in one of the Toledo-area cases. In this case, case 1, undercover investigations began in mid-2004 at a cluster of truck stops 20 miles from Harrisburg, Pennsylvania, known as the "Miracle Mile." According to investigators, Toledo women had been supplying prostitution services to this stretch of highway for years, yet prostitution cases were still dealt with one at a time. When such cases are discovered, police impound the trucks, and truckers are charged $400 to have them released from impound.

Central Pennsylvania local authorities, who at one time did not focus many resources on highway prostitution, became concerned about it when two bodies, both prostitutes, were found in the vicinity and a third, a 16-year-old prostitute, was thrown from a truck but survived. Adding to the call for action were rumors suggesting that a veteran local officer was accepting sexual favors to look the other way.

The officer was eventually convicted of two felony bribery charges. In the wake of these events, police officers and criminal justice students from local colleges started acting as decoy prostitutes in stings.

Similarly, at the Gables, a truck stop not far from the Miracle Mile and one of the focal points for the investigation, law enforcement dealt with one prostitute at a time rather than investigating the overall prostitution ring. There was so much demand that an individual prostitute could make more than $1,000 per night, so the $418 fine that had to be paid on arrest was considered an occupational expense. Prostitutes paid it and returned to the lot.

This transaction was as commonplace to the court staff who work for the local magistrate who administers these cases as it was to the prostitutes. However, after Pennsylvania state police began working with federal officials to crack down on prostitution, money from court fines increased nearly tenfold. In 2003, the township collected $3,319 in fines for prostitution, vandalism, or trespassing. The next year, fines jumped to $32,430.

Instead of treating prostitution as a string of petty crimes, as was done at the Miracle Mile and the Gables, investigators in the case started to view it as organized crime, convictions for which can carry life sentences. One Pennsylvania state trooper used a binder with photos to sort out the names and faces associated with the investigation. As early as 2002, he began sharing the photos with Ohio law enforcement, hoping to identify the prostitutes, who said that they did not work near Toledo because they were local and could thus be more easily identified.

Pennsylvania state police reportedly called the federal authorities for help when they could not thwart the problem. This brought the FBI, the Internal Revenue Service, U.S. postal inspectors, and federal prosecutors together for a coordinated response involving phone taps, traces of wire transfers, and questioning of the women and girls arrested for prostitution.

Federal prosecutors say that tracking prostitution rings is similar to other organized crime cases, in that the key is to "follow the money." An FBI analyst developed a database and tracked prostitutes and pimps. In 2005, the FBI hired 16 new agents to work on similar cases across the country.

Factors That Facilitate Investigation and Prosecution

As the case above illustrates and as respondents contend, collaboration is critical to investigating and prosecuting cases. Often, local authorities can do little to deal with human-trafficking rings on their own. All they could do in the case described above was move the prostitution problem out of one trucking rest stop. Likewise, without the cooperation of the Toledo-area authorities, the Pennsylvania state police could not identify victims of human trafficking transported to the community from Toledo. Furthermore, without the resources and expertise of the federal government, the Pennsylvania state police could not make a case that would come with federal penalties. And, finally, without the work of local officials, the federal government would not know that this was a problem.

Collaboration around the issue of human trafficking in Columbus is informal and relies on one-to-one relationships. There are no task forces or established collaborations to deal with this issue, although federal funding may have been available for one. Respondents agreed that local law enforcement personnel work well together on issues involving the investigation and prosecution of specific cases (for example, the Asian brothel cases described in Appendix D, which involved the collaboration of several local law enforcement agencies) but said that there is no systematic, ongoing coordination around types of cases, including those involving juvenile prostitutes. Further, some agencies tend to limit inter- and even intradepartment collaboration around these issues. As for local-federal partnerships, many local law enforcement officials perceive federal law enforcement officials to be too busy or unconcerned with these issues, although federal law enforcement officials contend that they are open to partnering with locals on these issues. Despite the fragmentation of partnerships in Columbus, most respondents indicated that they knew whom to call to initiate an investigation of human trafficking if there was a need. For many, this is a single person who has taken a lead role on the issue, which raises the question of sustainability of response in his or her absence.

Alternatively, in Toledo, there appears to be significant formal and informal collaboration around the issue of human trafficking. In August 2006, Toledo established a federal task force on human trafficking. Some respondents felt that the presence of a federally funded task force has made significant changes in how this issue is understood and managed. The task force includes representatives from the Toledo Police Department, other local police departments, the Lucas County Sheriff's Office, and the FBI. There is also a U.S. Attorney's Office liaison assigned to the task force. The task force provides resources for law enforcement, including support for personnel, overtime, equipment, and computer forensic support. These resources also allow for cross-deputization and a tight partnership between federal and local law enforcement. Federal authorities are interested in using the Mann Act (36 Stat. 825, 1910)[1] to prosecute trafficking that involves adults and the TVPA to prosecute trafficking that involves juveniles. Together, as part of six concrete cases counted in this analysis, this task force is currently tracking or investigating 60 potential traffickers.

Others in Toledo suggest that the relationship with federal law enforcement is a one-way street. Federal authorities want access to the victims, facilities, and information, but they provide little feedback to local practitioners. All agree that federal law enforcement agencies are anxious to prosecute these crimes and are very responsive to leads about possible victims, but the collaboration ends there, without services for the victims or appreciation for how the juvenile justice system works.

There is also a collaborative called the Prostitution Roundtable, which serves as a monthly forum for service providers, survivors, community members, law enforcement, and others to come together to discuss issues related to human trafficking. These monthly meetings have attendance levels of 50 to 75 people.

In addition to the formal collaboration, significant informal collaborations exist among the various players, who have a high degree of

---

[1]   The Mann Act prohibits "knowingly transport[ing] any individual in interstate or foreign commerce, or in any Territory or Possession of the United States, with intent that such individual engage in prostitution, or in any sexual activity for which any person can be charged with a criminal offense, or attempt[ing] to do so." This crime is punishable by a fine or imprisonment of not more than 10 years, or both.

knowledge of key players and their roles in the process. There appear to be partnerships in place to identify and handle human-trafficking cases with juveniles involved in commercial sex acts in Toledo. There seem to be few mechanisms in place to deal with other types of human trafficking in Toledo, but the evidence we found did not indicate problems with other types.

Factors That Impede Investigation and Prosecution

A consensus that emerged in our interviews was that lack of awareness, training, resources, and policies, as well as a desire to protect juvenile prostitutes and breakdowns between the juvenile justice and child welfare systems, impede investigations and prosecutions.

In four of five labor-trafficking cases, service providers indicated that, although they knew whom in law enforcement to contact about their trafficking victims, they could not take the chance that the disclosure could lead to negative consequences for their clients. A service provider reported that there are no examples of handling these cases successfully, and, as such, it is hard to trust a system that has not been tested. In addition, some respondents indicated that law enforcement's dual role of interrogating possible illegal immigrants on the one hand and helping exploited victims on the other hand creates a trust problem in many communities. Finally, it seems clear that law enforcement agencies must develop deeper inroads into these communities if they expect to be trusted.

For sex-trafficking cases, despite changes in the way Toledo deals with potential human-trafficking victims, the volume of cases—for example, the volume of cases of runaways who may be trafficking victims—seems to limit law enforcement's ability to respond. One respondent suggested that the policy of the local police on runaways is to wait for them to run back, even when there are obvious signs of possible foul play. This issue was illustrated in case 3, which involved Toledo-area girls who were abducted into a sex-trafficking ring. In this case, one victim was rescued by Michigan law enforcement, while the other was returned to a Toledo-area house.

The Michigan officials called the Toledo Police Department and outlined the case, suggesting that "this is not just a runaway . . . and the missing girl's father seemed upset enough to act on his own." The two officers spoke four times that day but the offender's name was an alias and the Toledo detective did not have a full address for the house. This lack of information was enough to prevent further investigation for a reportedly understaffed department with only two missing-person detectives.

With no action from local police, the parents reached the house. The father made his first call more than 90 minutes before police arrived; 911 logged three more calls from the family, plus numerous appeals from horrified neighbors. The father was so enraged, he reportedly could not wait any longer. He stormed the house, pretending that he had a gun and a fight ensued. The other victim was apparently shoved out of a second-story window, and, when police arrived a short time later, they untangled the bloodied adults, sending the two parents to the hospital and the three offenders to jail.

The response in this case illustrates resource constraints and priorities not uncommon in urban police departments. "For cops the monotony of runaway complaints—especially the chronic offenders police call 'frequent fliers'—can become white noise compared with robberies, car crashes, and murders" (de Boer and Erb, 2006a, p. A1). The Toledo Police Department used to have seven full-time detectives who tracked missing persons, but now there are only two detectives to investigate about 2,200 cases per year.

Furthermore, a possible desire to protect juvenile prostitutes may hinder their identification, as well as the investigation and prosecution of cases. Twenty-five years ago, the system used to charge juveniles with prostitution, but then, according to many (n = 5) of the respondents, those charges disappeared and were replaced with charges of loitering, disorderly conduct, being a runaway, probation violation, and status offenses, making the victims difficult to identify. Respondents said that they do not know why this happened, but they speculated that it had to do with a desire by law enforcement officials to protect the individuals involved.

Finally, breakdowns between the juvenile justice and child welfare systems in both Toledo and Columbus may hinder the identification of victims of human trafficking, which, in turn, will hinder investigations and prosecutions.

Charges and Penalties

The charges and penalties in cases for which information is known (four out of the 10 Toledo-based cases) are similar across cases. All but one of these cases was handled at the federal level, and charges included sex trafficking in children; taking minors across state lines for the purposes of prostitution; kidnapping; conspiracy; racketeering; tampering with a witness, victim, or informant; money laundering; sex conduct with a minor; and compelling underage prostitution. Albanese, Donnelly, and Kelegian (2004) also reported racketeering charges levied against human traffickers in the cases they identified; they found smuggling, conspiracy, or a combination of these charges utilized as well.

The possible penalties in the cases we identified included up to life in prison, $250,000 in fines for each conviction, and up to $1 million in forfeitures. The actual penalties include a 27-year-old Toledo man being sentenced to 40 years in federal prison (case 1). In case 2, a male trafficker was sentenced to 25 years in federal prison, and the female trafficker who assisted him pled guilty to sex trafficking and will serve 46 months in federal prison. In case 4, the trafficker was sentenced to 20 to 50 years in state prison. In the last case for which information is known (one of cases 5 through 10; see Appendix C for details), the offender faces a minimum five-year mandatory sentence in federal prison.

At the national level, federal prosecutions have increased in number for trafficking-related offenses. From 2001 to 2006, DOJ (2007) prosecuted 360 defendants, compared to 89 defendants charged during the prior six years, representing a more than 300-percent increase, and secured 238 convictions and guilty pleas, a 250-percent increase from the 67 obtained in the previous six years.

In addition to specifically combating child sex trafficking in the United States, DOJ identified 24 field offices with high incidences of child prostitution. These offices, which include Toledo, were given additional resources to combat the problem. As of September 30, 2005, these efforts had resulted in 139 open investigations, 505 arrests, 60 complaints, 70 indictments, and 67 convictions (DOJ, 2006).

Of the 25 defendants convicted under one of the statutes listed in the TVPA, as required to be reported by the U.S. Attorney General, 23 received a prison term. The average prison term imposed was 103 months, and terms ranged from 14 to 270 months (DOJ, 2006). Ten received a prison sentence of one to five years, five received terms of five to 10 years, and eight received a prison term of more than 10 years.

The Role of Criminal Statutes

There is considerable debate in the case study sites and in the literature about the benefit of federal versus state laws and penalties to deal with human-trafficking cases.

With the encouragement, assistance, and in some cases pressure of the Polaris Project, the Center for Women Policy Studies, and federal agencies such as DOJ, some 29 states have enacted antitrafficking statutes as of this writing.

According to advocates such as Schauer and Wheaton (2006), these laws give local police the tools necessary to be actively involved in the detection, arrest, and prosecution of traffickers, as well as in the rescuing and reintegration of sex-trafficking victims. Such advocates suggest that new state trafficking laws are necessary to stem the tide of human trafficking. Local and state police are handicapped by antiquated prostitution statutes. They respond to trafficking-related behaviors according to a prostitution paradigm that treats victims as offenders. Schauer and Wheaton (2006) note, further, that many states do not criminalize the actions of customers, pimps, and transporters of women, nor business owners. One of the goals of these new laws is to move local and state law enforcement from a prostitution paradigm to a human-trafficking paradigm that will increase the detection of victims and the prosecution of offenders.

One of the reservations to enacting state laws has been the idea that human trafficking is a federal problem and, thus, not something to be made the subject of state jurisdiction (Finckenauer and Liu, 2006). For example, more than 70 percent of local law enforcement agencies indicated that human trafficking is a problem best addressed by federal law enforcement (Wilson, Walsh, and Kleuber, 2006). Despite the push for and enactment of state laws to combat human trafficking, there had been no state prosecutions of trafficking cases as of October 2006 (Finckenauer and Liu, 2006).

As with the literature, opinions about whether human trafficking is a local or federal problem are varied. Some criminal justice and social service provider respondents (n = 9) suggested that federal laws and penalties are key to prosecuting human-trafficking cases. They see federal involvement as necessary because the federal government has the resources to pursue these cases, particularly the ability to investigate cases that cross jurisdictional boundaries. Other respondents felt that the victims would not cooperate with the prosecution if they knew that their trafficker would get a short prison sentence or no sentence at all. Long federal sentences make the victims feel protected. At least one other respondent suggested that there are not enough cases to justify a state response.

However, five criminal justice respondents (two in Columbus and three in Toledo) suggested that the state law will improve response and put more power in the hands of local agencies, where the cases should be handled. According to these respondents, federal prosecutions take so long that, by the time they are complete, another generation of victims has suffered.

Columbus and Toledo Comparison

As is clear from the descriptions presented in this chapter, the response to juvenile sex-trafficking cases in Columbus differs considerably from that in Toledo. In Columbus, there is almost no awareness that human trafficking can involve juveniles in commercial sex transactions from which an adult benefits. This lack of awareness, coupled with lack of resources, lack of local-federal law enforcement collaboration, lack of dedicated staff or a dedicated unit to handle trafficking cases, and lack of systematic community–service provider partnerships, leads to handling potential human-trafficking victims as offenders, which may partly lead to the lack of identified human-trafficking cases in the jurisdiction.

In Toledo, the criminal justice community has made significant changes to promote awareness, identification, and investigation of human-trafficking cases. Federal resources and collaborations among federal, state, and local law enforcement agencies and service providers have helped facilitate this change. These changes have likely led to the increase in the number of cases investigated and prosecuted in Toledo involving Toledo-area actors.

In both Toledo and Columbus, respondents reported a disconnect between the justice system's and the child welfare system's responses, which may hinder the investigation and prosecution of cases.

Law enforcement authorities were made aware of only one of the few known labor-trafficking cases in Columbus, and there were no known cases in Toledo. However, law enforcement respondents in both communities suggested that they would respond to such cases if they were made aware of them.

CHAPTER FOUR

Service Provider and Community Responses

Beyond understanding how the justice system responds to human trafficking in the two sites, we also wanted to understand how service providers and the communities in each site respond to it. This chapter discusses that response, seeking to describe victims' critical needs so that policymakers and practitioners have a clearer understanding of how they might improve their assistance to trafficking victims. The analysis is based primarily on interviews with individuals working for service providers in the two case study sites but also relies on the content analysis.

Here, we discuss the response, beginning first with a discussion of who the providers are and what services they provide and then moving on to discuss training and resources, meeting victim needs, and collaboration. We conclude, as we did in the previous chapters, with a comparison of the response between the two case study sites.

Service Providers and Services Provided

Three of the eight social service organizations (two prostitution recovery service providers in Toledo and one immigrant and refugee service provider in Columbus) reported dealing with victims of human trafficking as defined by the TVPA, although the other service providers in Toledo also reported knowledge of the existence of human-trafficking victims.

One of these two prostitution recovery service providers reported working with 12 trafficking victims from 2006 to early 2007, eight of whom are cooperating with federal investigations. These girls are most often identified through street outreach efforts. The other prostitution recovery provider suggested that there may be about six cases each year but that each of these girls has two or three friends who are also involved. The organization also works with about 50 adult women per year, nearly half of whom started prostituting before they turned 18. The immigrant and refugee service provider in Columbus has worked with three to four labor exploitation and trafficking victims in recent years but suggested that there are more who have not been identified.

In addition to the nonprofit and community-based service providers, the juvenile justice system in Toledo attempts to serve juvenile sex-trafficking victims by providing family counseling and addressing mental health, substance abuse, and other needs. However, at the time of this study, these services were not necessarily population-specific. This is because the juvenile justice system must contract with proven treatment and placement programs for juvenile victims of human trafficking. The respondents advised that none of the programs had been evaluated sufficiently to meet their criteria.

Training and Resources

Most of the service providers and community-based organizations (six of eight) indicated that staff had received training or conducted training on human trafficking. The training ranged from local presentations and conferences to training sponsored by the federal government and national nonprofit organizations. This is a much higher percentage of training than was reported by service providers surveyed (11 percent) in a national needs assessment of service providers and trafficking victims conducted by Caliber Associates (Clawson et al., 2003). However, our sample is not necessarily representative of all agencies, because we selected them based on their likely involvement in human trafficking, if it exists.

Three of the service providers reported receiving resources or fee-for-service contracts to treat victims of human trafficking. The funding ranged from one Toledo-based prostitution recovery provider receiving support from a national organization and private funders to another Toledo-based prostitution recovery program receiving a contract with the child welfare agency to treat families with prostitution or sex-trafficking issues. However, with this contract, very little of the money is spent, reportedly because of the quick closure of cases and the contract stipulations, which do not provide resources for tracking down victims, only for face-to-face services. Finally, a service provider that offers services to immigrant populations in Columbus is a subgrantee of a federal government grant to the U.S. Conference of Catholic Bishops, an organization that has a subgrantee in each state to provide services to both certified and uncertified victims of human trafficking. The contract is fee for service, and there are different rates depending on the victim's official certification status.

At the national level, the U.S. Department of State has funded anti-trafficking programs in 50 countries. The U.S. Department of Health and Human Services has provided grant funding to 28 service providers throughout the country to provide education, outreach, and direct assistance to trafficking victims. Finally, DOJ's Office of Victims of Crime (OVC) has awarded 27 grants funding 25 direct service projects for victims, one project that provides technical assistance to OVC trafficking grantees, and one that focuses on building shelter capacity for trafficking victims. During 2005, OVC's grantees provided services to 682 victims, up from 357 in the previous calendar year, bringing the number of victims served since the inception of the program to 1,184 (DOJ, 2006).

Meeting the Needs of Victims

Victim Needs

All respondents that had experience with the issue indicated that sex and labor trafficking victims have significant needs, starting with major trauma, depression, and safety concerns (n = 11). Other problems include physical abuse, substance use, mental health, physical health, education, housing, employment, and other concerns. This is consistent with research in this area specifically indicating that many women in the sex industry experience depression, have suicidal thoughts, have tried to hurt or kill themselves, have had head injuries, feel hopelessness and rage, and use drugs or alcohol (Estes and Weiner, 2001). A national survey of service providers that work with trafficking victims suggests that the greatest needs of sex-trafficking victims include legal services, medical services, and information or referral services (Clawson et al., 2003).

In addition, support services used by street youth who exited the sex industry include assistance in dealing with law enforcement, assistance in dealing with pimps and traffickers, street-based outreach services, child care, family reunification services, health services, legal services, services to help them in having nonsexual relationships with caring adults, housing, substance abuse treatment, and employment training.

Many of these services are available, but respondents contend that they are not adequately funded. One or both prostitution recovery service providers in Toledo provide assistance in dealing with law enforcement, assistance in dealing with pimps and traffickers, street-based outreach services, and assistance in having nonsexual relationships with caring adults. In addition, one or both have established or are in the process of establishing links to child care, family reunification services, health services, legal services, substance abuse treatment, and employment training services. Both providers indicated that more funding was necessary to treat victims.

The service provider assisting labor-trafficking victims in Columbus reported that these victims are among those most in need that they serve, and in many ways have needs that are similar to those of victims of domestic violence. Similar to what was found in Minnesota, these victims do not come in as trafficking victims but as individuals with other needs and whose trafficking becomes known only later as trust is developed between the provider and the client (Minnesota Statistical Analysis Center, 2006).

Ability to Respond to Victim Needs

While victims of trafficking have many resource needs, the service providers we interviewed said that they can handle the needs of victims and indicate a strong desire to reach more victims. These findings are echoed in the literature. Surveys of service providers find that, in general, most respondents contend that, with their existing resources and what they are able to piece together with the help of other providers, they are able to meet some of their victims' needs (Minnesota Statistical Analysis Center, 2006).

Service providers reported a significant need for shelter for both labor- and sex-trafficking victims—crisis, short-term, and long-term housing for trafficking victims. In Columbus, shelters are increasingly taking in only Columbus or Franklin County residents, leaving no safe places for those without a local residence. In Toledo, providers asserted that placements are difficult because, with few exceptions for serious offenders, they are not secure, which means the victims can—and will—just walk away.

One secure placement option does exist in Toledo, to which judges refer victims, as appropriate. Here, victims receive up to 18 months of intensive treatment for all of their needs—including mental health, substance abuse, and trauma disorders. In addition, one of the prostitution recovery providers was in the process of establishing housing for this population. Finally, the federal government has housing for victims and witnesses of human trafficking, but these options are not frequently used and are located far from Ohio.

In addition to housing, shelter, and secure placements, suggested services include a drop-in center; crisis line; more outreach; more involvement of survivors in the criminal justice, outreach, and healing processes; and more population-specific treatment. A "Johns' school" that intervenes with those who solicit prostitutes to limit the demand for sex trafficking was offered as another need. A respondent explained that one is being planned in Columbus.

Barriers to Accessing Services
In the literature, barriers to accessing services include fear of retaliation, lack of knowledge about services, fear of deportation, lack of social support, lack of trust in the system, language differences, lack of knowledge about rights, feelings of shame, general fear, and not being able to identify oneself as a victim (Minnesota Statistical Analysis

Center, 2006). Several respondents (n = 6) noted these same barriers and also indicated a need to have survivors reach out to victims to walk them through the process, as well as a need to ensure that providers and law enforcement agencies treat victims with respect and care.

System Gaps

Several respondents (n = 6) discussed the system breakdown that occurs between the child welfare and juvenile justice systems in treating juvenile victims of sex trafficking. Many said that the child welfare system is unlikely to open a case and is quick to close a case, often with evidence of prostitution by juveniles or their parents. Respondents gave several explanations for this, including training and education needs, funding issues, high caseloads, and the perception that these juveniles should be handled by the justice system. Many suggested that the Family First Council in Toledo is the appropriate body to address the gaps between the child welfare and the juvenile justice systems.

Another problem highlighted in Toledo is the protocol for investigating runaways. Apparently, runaways are treated as missing persons, and investigations of them are not pursued aggressively. Those we interviewed believed that, if runaways were treated as possible human-trafficking victims or victims of other crime, the system would be more effective in dealing with the problem.

Further, service providers in Toledo admit that the majority of their efforts and services are set up to support juvenile and adult victims of domestic sex trafficking but not sex trafficking involving Hispanic, Asian, or other international victims or labor trafficking. They do not have strong networks in Asian or other foreign communities that may have trafficking victims. They do not know about providers to serve these populations. These same providers apparently do not have the resources to reach a Spanish-only–speaking or other non–English-speaking community.

Finally, a respondent from the provider servicing labor-trafficking victims in Columbus suggested that many policies regarding illegal immigrants, such as those that do not allow non-U.S. citizens to access services, are significant barriers to adequate service delivery.

Collaboration

As providers have gained more knowledge about the elements necessary to meet the needs of trafficking victims, they have also realized that no one agency can do it alone (Clawson et al., 2003). Service providers must collaborate to piece their existing services together in an attempt to provide trafficking victims with the unique blend of services they require.

In their national survey, Caliber found that respondents report collaborating to share information, resources, and staff and to provide and receive training (Clawson et al., 2003). Group types likeliest to collaborate include human-trafficking victim and survivor advocacy groups, domestic violence groups, victim assistance groups, health services, police, attorneys, faith communities, housing providers, district attorneys, and educational institutions.

In Toledo, service providers, community members, survivors, activists, law enforcement officials, and others convene monthly to discuss issues related to human trafficking, primarily sex trafficking. This collaboration, called the Prostitution Roundtable, often involves 50 to 75 attendees and allows for discussion of issues related to sex trafficking. The meeting topics vary, but they have included new legislation, establishing support systems, and improving prevention.

Connections between service providers and law enforcement are key to effective justice system responses. Bales and Lize (2005) found that service providers are critical to stabilizing victims to the point at which they are able to cooperate with law enforcement. This type of partnership seems to exist between one of the prostitution recovery service providers and the FBI. The provider shares significant information about potential victims with the FBI, working closely with federal law enforcement to assist in making cases. While the provider's main objective is to work with the victims and they report that trust is fragile yet key to the partnership, they also seem anxious to bring traffickers to justice and therefore support federal efforts to do so.

Columbus and Toledo Comparison

There was little observance of human-trafficking cases in Columbus. As such, little response was seen by service providers or by the criminal justice community, with the exception of the one provider we interviewed who has seen a few victims of labor exploitation. Moreover, there is little awareness of possible juvenile sex-trafficking victims in Columbus, despite the broad consideration of the issue in Toledo. Despite this, respondents in Columbus indicated that, if they identified a human-trafficking victim, they would make partnerships and use their existing networks to serve him or her.

However, as discussed earlier, there has been a considerable reaction and response to juvenile trafficking victims by the community in Toledo. While programs are still small and struggling and may be prepared to address only one type of possible human-trafficking victim, the community in Toledo has a comparatively organized and collaborative approach to dealing with human-trafficking victims.

As such, the only similarity found between the two case study sites was the need for more shelter options for victims of human trafficking and the disconnect between the child welfare and juvenile justice systems' treatment of children and families with possible connections to human trafficking.

CHAPTER FIVE

Key Policy Considerations

Our analysis focused on describing the human-trafficking market, as well as how the criminal justice and social service communities are reacting to human trafficking, in two case study sites in Ohio. Using an evidence-based approach, we focused on cases for which evidence existed to support their classification as human trafficking according to the TVPA definition. We base the discussion in this chapter on these concrete cases.

Given the relatively small number of cases we identified, policy-makers and practitioners must carefully weigh their response to this crime relative to other priorities. As with all public safety (and other) investments, there is an opportunity cost to resources that must be considered. Although all crime inherently warrants a response, providing resources, in whatever form, to more effectively address one type of offense necessarily limits resources that can be used to address another.

Despite the small number of concrete cases we identified, there are several reasons that warrant, at a minimum, further discussion about response options. First, as explained in Chapter One, our identification of concrete cases should be interpreted as a minimum baseline or lower-bound estimate of human trafficking. It is possible that additional cases exist in other areas of Ohio, perhaps even in Columbus and Toledo, or that cases involving victims and offenders from Ohio appear elsewhere in the United States. Second, each case can involve numerous victims and offenders (the six cases currently being investigated in Toledo involve as many as 60 traffickers). Third, this offense has existed as a crime only since 2000, and changing the traditional practices (e.g., from processing prostitutes as offenders to treating them as victims) takes both time and training. Finally, human trafficking is a clandestine crime; increasing resources for and awareness of it will likely coincide with the identification of more cases. For policymakers and practitioners who want to improve on the current response to human trafficking, our analysis provides insight into several areas that could be considered. We describe these in this remainder of this chapter.

Improve Awareness and Response Through Training, Education, and Outreach

There is a need for greater awareness of human trafficking among the general public, potential first responders (including child welfare caseworkers, doctors, nurses, hospital personnel, law enforcement officials, teachers, and school resource officers), parents, prosecutors and defense attorneys, and other criminal and juvenile justice system personnel. There is widespread agreement that training to make stakeholders more aware of human trafficking increases the number of cases identified. Therefore, to better identify and serve the needs of victims and investigate and prosecute offenders, training should be expanded to include all stakeholders.

Human-trafficking awareness training could be provided in two parts. First, all stakeholders could receive the same general awareness information, such as how to identify human-trafficking victims, what types of cases exist and their typical fact patterns, and what to do and whom to contact when victims are identified or suspicious activity is discovered.

Second, the training could include stakeholder-specific modules to give each group information relevant to its role. For example, training for law enforcement could include information on available social service programs for victims, questions to investigate in suspected human-trafficking cases, and the legal elements of human trafficking and the evidence required to support them (for example, many law enforcement respondents felt that some crimes that involved criminal networks were human trafficking, even though the characteristics they described did not by themselves qualify the crimes as human trafficking). Training for health service staff could include characteristics and warning signs associated with victims of human trafficking when they seek medical attention.

More generally, outreach and education could also be used to improve the awareness of the community at large with regard to human trafficking. Many human-trafficking cases have been discovered by a community member who saw something that "did not look right" and somehow intervened, such as by helping a victim or calling the police. Making the general public more aware of this crime may help to uncover more cases.

Some new awareness efforts are currently under way. According to one respondent, the U.S. Department of Health and Human Services is increasing the number of rescue and restore coalitions from 16 to 20, with Columbus serving as a location for a new coalition. Part of the effort will be to train the community and conduct outreach. Also, at the time of this study, a regional training center in Toledo was planning to conduct its first event.

Improve Victim Programs and Resources

There are a several specific areas for which more services for human-trafficking victims are needed. According to respondents, needs include a drop-in center, safe havens, secure placements, short- and long-term aftercare housing options that allow for intensive population-specific treatment, a crisis line, and improved outreach to victims (e.g., through a MySpace™ Web page). Respondents also felt that more evidence-based, population-specific treatment options were needed at every stage in the recovery process. Treatment and outreach should also include survivors in the process. Finally, respondents reported a need for philosophies and programs to understand and develop ways to address the root causes of human trafficking.

Improve Law Enforcement Capacity

To tackle these large and time-intensive investigations, law enforcement respondents advise that they need more personnel and overtime resources. Human-trafficking investigations consume significant amounts of time and are low-yield in terms of prosecution. More resources would allow for dedicated staff to identify more cases and investigate them more thoroughly. Likewise, as law enforcement officials contend, there is value in thoroughly investigating various case types that do not initially appear to be human trafficking but that could be found to be trafficking on more extensive inquiry or that could at least provide lessons that would inform human-trafficking cases. Either way, more thorough investigation of such cases could potentially uncover greater criminal networks. These investigations are also labor-intensive and require dedicated, sustained resources. Dedicated staff can also spread responsibility and increase the ability to provide a seamless response in the absence of any particular staff member. (As noted above, the response in Columbus is largely coordinated through a single person.)

Improve Practitioner Collaboration

Although positive signs exist, there is a clear need for greater collaboration, most notably among the law enforcement community. There is a widespread need for collaboration among local law enforcement, federal investigators, and prosecutors of all levels. Respondents generally agreed that federal investigators and prosecutors could work more cooperatively with others in the law enforcement community. For some practitioners, the relationship with federal law enforcement is a one-way street: Federal authorities want access to the victims, facilities, and information, but they provide little feedback to local practitioners. All respondents agreed that federal law enforcement is anxious to prosecute these crimes and is very responsive to leads about possible victims, but many contended that the collaboration ends there, without services for the victims or an appreciation for how the local juvenile justice system works.

Collaboration also needs to be improved within agencies. This is most evident in Columbus, for example, where different units of the Columbus Division of Police share responsibility for investigating human-trafficking and associated cases. Although it is apparently improving, greater communication could help improve coordination.

Refine Departmental Policies

There are at least three system changes that could improve the identification and response to human trafficking. First, there is a need for a screening process and standard protocol for law enforcement officers to follow when interacting with potential human-trafficking victims. This process needs to be victim-centered rather than treat victims as offenders.

Second, jurisdictional issues exist such that some local shelters will serve only residents of a specific county. This excludes many possible human-trafficking victims, further limiting their housing options. Generally speaking, to the extent that service provision is limited to victims meeting certain qualifications because of funding-source restrictions, other support systems (e.g., state and federal grants) could help overcome these limitations.

Third, there are breakdowns between the child welfare and the juvenile justice systems. For example, juvenile prostitutes are generally charged with lesser offenses. This approach treats these potential human-trafficking victims as criminals and makes it difficult to track these individuals. There also was interest in improving the response to runaways, who are currently perceived to be low priority for local police, because this may be an important way to identify trafficking victims.

Use Analyses to Develop Evidence-Based Programs and Responses

A substantial body of criminal justice research demonstrates that specific, data-driven interventions and programs tailored to a specific problem are more effective at addressing problems than investing resources and responding in ways that do not reflect a solid understanding of the problem and its underlying characteristics. Recognizing this, respondents indicated the need for more research and information on human trafficking. By providing examples of known cases of human trafficking and how criminal justice authorities and social service providers are responding it, our analysis provides a first step in this direction and informs decisionmaking in regard to human-trafficking policy and programs.

In addition, this analysis can also be used to shape subsequent inquiries. For example, it would be useful to learn why the human-trafficking markets in Columbus and Toledo appear to be different based on the few concrete cases and whether Ohio's other urban communities, such as Cleveland and Cincinnati, differ in their experience with human trafficking relative to what we discovered in Columbus and Toledo. Likewise, it would be helpful to explore this issue in Ohio's rural communities, where it has received little attention. Drawing from the baseline information in this monograph, it would be possible to conduct a statewide survey of various stakeholder groups to learn their experiences with the issues identified in our analysis and to identify their needs. Analyses that draw directly on those involved in the trafficking process—victims, offenders, and associates—would also offer insight into developing programs for victims and investigating offenders. Finally, it would be instructive to examine the process, challenges, successes, and lessons of the current federally funded human-trafficking task force in Toledo.

Consider and Assess Legislative, Legal, and Regulatory Changes

The perceived utility of the pending state legislation to strengthen laws and penalties in human-trafficking cases was mixed. On the one hand, respondents believed the state law will improve response by placing more power in the hands of local officials. In addition to the difficulties of working with federal prosecutors, some respondents said that federal prosecutions take so long that, by the time they are complete, another generation of victims has suffered. On the other hand, other respondents felt that there may not be a need for a state law because of the small volume of cases and because of their belief that such cases are better handled at the federal level. At the very least, it appears that state legislation would provide the law enforcement community an additional tool to use in combating human trafficking, possibly increasing the number of cases investigated and prosecuted.

Despite this debate about state legislation, several more specific legal and regulatory recommendations arose from our analysis. First, victims view the federal human-trafficking certification process with suspicion, most notably because they could provide information that puts their and their families' safety at risk without any guarantee that they will be certified and receive services. As part of a state legislative package, legislators could consider creating a state certification process that overcomes the limitations in the federal certification process and entitles victims to immediate, comprehensive, state-supported services, which include access to safe housing facilities. Respondents reported that domestic victims are most in need of these services because they have fewer options than immigrant victims, who can receive services through the U.S. Department of Health and Human Services.

Second, there is need for stricter licensing and inspection of massage parlors, spas, clinics, hotels, and other places that may employ many foreign-born workers. The concrete cases of human trafficking we identified did not include these kinds of establishments, but many respondents felt that they could be related to human trafficking. Similarly, respondents felt that there should be better mechanisms to prosecute the owners of the establishments if they are found to house illegal businesses.

Finally, federal immigration laws (including those under consideration) should be examined relative to potential impacts on human trafficking. For example, the Real ID Act of 2005 (contained in P.L. 109-13) is an attempt to enhance the validity and consistency of state-issued identification documents. A respondent claimed that this act could increase immigrant workers' reliance on traffickers who can transport them, which could lead to their further exploitation. Our analysis cannot speak to the overall efficacy of this or other immigrations laws, but it suggests that their implications should be carefully thought out.

Background Information on Case Study Sites

In this appendix, we provide background information on each of the case study sites.

Columbus, Ohio

Columbus is the largest city in Ohio and the 15th largest in the United States (Columbus Chamber of Commerce, undated). Columbus is the seat of Franklin County and the state capital. Unlike many other Midwest cities, Columbus continues to expand its reach through annexations and extensions, making it one of the fastest-growing large cities in the nation, both in terms of land area and population. Because of its central location, nearly all of Ohio is within a two-hour drive of Columbus. Likewise, Detroit, Chicago, Nashville, Pittsburgh, St. Louis, Toronto, and Washington, D.C., are all less than an eight-hour drive from Columbus.

In 2000, Columbus was composed of a largely white (68 percent) and black (24 percent) population but also included significant proportions of Hispanics (nearly 2.5 percent and growing) and Asians (3.5 percent); in addition, 10 percent of the population spoke a language other than English at home (U.S. Census Bureau, 2007a). The current immigration wave includes an influx of people from India, China, eastern Africa (especially Somalia), Mexico, and other Latin American countries. From 2000 to 2003, international immigration accounted for 82 percent of Franklin County's net population growth (Pyle, 2006). The Ohio State University, which has the single largest international student population in the country, helps to draw individuals from nearly all nations and cultures to study in Columbus. About 15 percent of the population was below the poverty line in 2000.

Columbus has the strongest economy in Ohio ("Study: Columbus Has Ohio's Best Economy," 2006). The largest employers include the government (federal, state, and local), institutions of higher education, the insurance industry, and the mortgage and banking industry. Many technology companies also have headquarters or major corporate offices in Columbus. Columbus is home to the Defense Supply Center. As part of the Defense Logistics Agency, it procures $642 million each year in supplies and is known throughout the world as the largest supplier of weapon system spare parts (GlobalSecurity.org. 2005).

Toledo, Ohio

The city of Toledo is located in northwestern Ohio and is the seat of Lucas County. The city sits 75 miles east of the Ohio-Indiana border and borders Michigan to the north and Lake Erie to the east. Toledo is the fourth-largest city in Ohio and the 57th largest in the United States. Toledo's population has been declining since the 1970s, when the census counted almost 384,000 people—down about 70,000 to 314,000 in 2000 (U.S. Census Bureau, 2007b).

The city has convenient access to three of the country's most traveled interstates, I-80, I-90, and I-75. Sitting at these major crossroads, Toledo's location has allowed it to have the third most active rail hubs in the United States and made it a center for the trucking industry. The Toledo Express Airport is the 15th-busiest cargo airport in the nation, is home to the busiest passenger rail terminal, and has been recognized as one of the most diversified and busiest international cargo facilities (Hoemann, 2005).

In 2000, Toledo was composed of a largely white (70 percent) and black (24 percent) population; however, nearly 5.5 percent (and growing) of the population was Hispanic, and 7 percent spoke a language other than English at home (U.S. Census Bureau, 2007b). About 18 percent of the population was below the poverty line in 2000.

Toledo is well known for manufacturing. The big three automakers—General Motors, Ford, and Daimler-Chrysler—all have factories and are continuing to expand in metropolitan Toledo (City of Toledo, 2006). The city is home to three Fortune 500 companies: Dana Corporation, Owens Corning, and Owens-Illinois.

Content Analysis References

In this appendix, we list references for the articles collected in the content analysis, drawn from the *Columbus Dispatch* and the *Toledo Blade*.

Columbus Dispatch

Articles Referencing Concrete Cases of Human Trafficking (0)

Articles Referencing Cases Constructive for Human Trafficking (13)

Cadwallader, Bruce, "Convicted Madam Agrees to Testify Against Other; Woman Who Faced $1 Billion Bail Is Released After She Pleads Guilty," *Columbus Dispatch*, August 4, 2005, p. 10C.

Carmen, Barbara, "Twice-Raided Storefront; 2 Workers Charged with Prostitution at North Side Spa," *Columbus Dispatch*, January 28, 2006, p. 7B.

Cervantes, Alice, "Brothel Arrests: Asian Spas Only Work Some Women Have Known," *Columbus Dispatch*, July 3, 2005, p. 1A.

Codispoti, Amanda, "Bail Set for More Women Charged in Brothel Case: One Woman's Bail Increased by $750,000," *Columbus Dispatch*, June 25, 2005, p. 5B.

DeMartini, Alayna, "Brothel Suspect's Bond at $1 Billion; Woman Among Four Charged After Raid on Massage Parlors," *Columbus Dispatch*, June 24, 2005, p. 1B.

———, "Raid Keeps Heat on North Side Massage Parlor," *Columbus Dispatch*, March 5, 2006, p. 2C.

Futty, John, "Two Women Arrested in Raid on Massage Parlor," *Columbus Dispatch*, July 15, 2005, p. 2C.

Marx, Matthew, "Three-State Indictment: Man Arrested in Job-Fraud Ring," *Columbus Dispatch*, April 12, 2006, p. 5B.

Mayhood, Kevin, "Alleged Immigration Scheme; Man Denies Bringing Mexicans in Illegally," *Columbus Dispatch*, March 14, 2004, p. 6C.

"North Side Asian Spas: 2nd Suspect in Brothel Case Free After Judge Reduces Bail," *Columbus Dispatch*, August 5, 2005, p. 5E.

"Police Seeking 7th Woman in Prostitution Case," *Columbus Dispatch*, June 30, 2005, p. 4C.

"Woman Charged in Sting Gets Probation: Massage Parlors Sold Sex, Police Say," *Columbus Dispatch*, September 30, 2005, p. 4B.

"Woman Indicted on Prostitution Charges Still at Large, Police Say," *Columbus Dispatch,* July 16, 2005, p. 6B.

Articles Referencing Background Information on Human Trafficking (10)

Goodenow, Evan, "Trafficking Seminar; Police Fear Central Ohio Ripe for Slave Trade," *Columbus Dispatch*, March 31, 2005, p. 9C.

Phillips, Jeb, "City Targeting Buildings with Illegal Activity: Landlords Warned to Tend to Property or Risk Padlocking, Police, Officials Say," *Columbus Dispatch*, February 19, 2006, p. 6C.

Pyle, Encarnacion, "Saved from Destruction; Recognizing Link Between Drugs, Prostitution, Maryhaven Program Helps Women Get Back Lives," *Columbus Dispatch*, April 19, 2006, p. 1E.

Richards, Kirk, "Prostitution Rare in Suburbs, Police Say: Dublin Arrest Shows Oldest Profession Not Just in Big Cities," *Columbus Dispatch*, August 21, 2004, p. 3B.

Riskind, Jonathan, "Ex–Sex Slave from Moldova Might Walk, U.S. Doctors Say," *Columbus Dispatch,* May 1, 2005, p. 6A.

———, "Anti–Sex-Trafficking Bill Expected to Pass in House," *Columbus Dispatch,* December 11, 2005, p. 8A.

———, "Pryce's Bill to Fight Sex Trafficking Becomes Law," *Columbus Dispatch*, January 11, 2006, p. 5A.

Torry, Jack, "Pryce to Travel with Group to Investigate Sex Trafficking," *Columbus Dispatch,* March 27, 2005, p. 11A.

———, "Sex Slave Brought to U.S. for Treatment: Pryce, Colleagues Worked to Help Teen After Trip to Moldova," *Columbus Dispatch*, April 23, 2005, p. 5A.

"Trip Reinforces Pryce's Fight Against Child-Sex Traffickers," *Columbus Dispatch*, April 10, 2005, p. 9A.

Toledo Blade

Articles Referencing Concrete Cases of Human Trafficking (28)

de Boer, Roberta, "A Teen Girl's Favorite Place Might Harbor Predators," *Toledo Blade*, October 2, 2003, p. B1.

de Boer, Roberta, and Robin Erb, "Reports of Runaways End Up at Bottom of Investigation Pile—Lack of Manpower, Parental Interest Deters Probes," *Toledo Blade*, February 12, 2006, p. A1.

————, "Surviving in Wayne's World," *Toledo Blade*, May 14, 2006, p. A1.

Erb, Robin, "Buffie Rae's Slaying Leaves Mom with Few Answers; Body Exhibited Telltale Marks of Violent End," *Toledo Blade*, January 8, 2006, p. A4.

————, "3 Women Allegedly Aided Pimp Suspect—Indictment Says Trio Hid Man from Agents," *Toledo Blade*, March 3, 2006, p. B1.

————, "Police Stings Curtail Prostitution at Harrisburg-Area Truck Stops," *Toledo Blade*, March 20, 2006, p. A1.

————, "Pimp Gets 25 Years for Kidnap, Sex Crimes—Ex-Toledoan Forced Teen into Prostitution," *Toledo Blade*, April 4, 2006, p. B1.

————, "Toledo Sex-Trade Case Sparks State, National Action," *Toledo Blade*, June 20, 2006, p. A1.

Erb, Robin, and Roberta de Boer, "Crackdown Exposes Toledo as a Hub of Teen Prostitution—Local Residents Provide Management, Muscle, Recruits for National Operation," *Toledo Blade,* January 8, 2006, p. A1.

————, "Captive Teenage Cousins Suffer Crash Course in Forced Sex Trade: Police Say Toledo Trio Enslaved 2 Girls Plucked from Busy City Street in May," *Toledo Blade*, January 9, 2006, p. A1.

————, "Dots on Sex-Trade Picture Largely Went Unconnected—Experts Say Pimps Adept at Luring Vulnerable Teens," *Toledo Blade*, January 10, 2006, p. A1.

————, "Girl Endured Brutal Journey Through World of Prostitution—Ex-Toledoan Faces Justice for Enslaving Adrian Teen," *Toledo Blade,* February 26, 2006, p. A1.

————, "Harrisburg Area Proved Profitable for Pimps, Prostitutes from Toledo—Arrests, Fines Viewed as Routine Part of Business," *Toledo Blade*, March 19, 2006, p. A1.

————, "Investigation Heralds New Era in Prostitution Fight—FBI Increasing Resources in Bid to Cut Off Supply Lines," *Toledo Blade*, March 19, 2006, p. A6.

————, "Prostitutes' 'Name Game' Scheme Often Obscures Extent of Sex Trade," *Toledo Blade*, April 23, 2006, p. A1.

————, "Teen Prostitute Found Dead Had Slipped Away Long Ago—Landmark Lakes Treaty May Be Reworked," *Toledo Blade*, May 8, 2006, p. A1.

————, "Bold Teenage Prostitute Wanted Out of 'the Game'—Toledoan Is Home Insisting She's Not Afraid," *Toledo Blade*, May 15, 2006, p. A1.

"Ex-Toledoan Guilty in Sex Case," *Toledo Blade*, October 20, 2004, p. B3.

"Kidnap Suspect Arraigned in Detroit—Adrian Teen Forced into Prostitution," *Toledo Blade*, February 5, 2005, p. B1.

"Kidnapper's Sentencing Delayed—Man Convicted of Abducting Adrian Teen Faces Life Term," *Toledo Blade*, February 28, 2006, p. B3.

McFeatters, Ann, and Mark Reiter, "31 Accused of Running Child Sex Ring—Many of the Young Girls 'Herded' Around Country Are from Toledo," *Toledo Blade*, December 17, 2005, p. A1.

Reiter, Mark, "Toledoan Linked to Prostitution Ring—Indictment Alleges Multistate Operation That Recruited Underage Girls," *Toledo Blade*, November 19, 2005, p. B1.

"Sentence in Prostitution Case Delayed," *Toledo Blade*, March 14, 2006, p. B2.

"3 Accused of Using Girls as Prostitutes," *Toledo Blade*, December 16, 2005, p. B4.

"3 Are Charged with Forcing Girls into Prostitution," *Toledo Blade*, May 25, 2005, p. B2.

"Toledo Man Sentenced to 40 Years for Role in U.S. Case," *Toledo Blade*, October 27, 2005, p. A3.

"Toledo Woman Found Dead—Body Left at Abandoned Truck Stop Near Indianapolis," *Toledo Blade*, March 26, 2004, p.B3.

"U.S. Authorities Want Help Finding Suspect in Prostitution Ring," *Toledo Blade*, February 11, 2006, p. B6.

Articles Referencing Cases Constructive for Human Trafficking (4)

Emch, Dale, "Pair Who Ran Sex Ring Must Give Up $1M," *Toledo Blade*, July 23, 2003, p. B1.

Murphy, Steve, "Crackdown on Massage Parlors Nets 9 Arrests—Lima Police File Prostitution Charges," *Toledo Blade*, October 28, 2004, p. B1.

"Prostitution Ring Member Is Sentenced," *Toledo Blade*, November 30, 2004, p. B2.

Vezner, Tad, "Prostitution Ring Forfeits Big Bucks to Government—More Than $500,000 Was Found in Homes," *Toledo Blade*, November 26, 2004, p. B1.

Articles Referencing Background Information on Human Trafficking (9)

Bates, Kim, "Topics of Prostitution, Sex—Industry Draw 250 to Forum at UT," *Toledo Blade*, September 24, 2004, p. B1.

de Boer, Roberta, "Even Before It Opens, Crisis Center Has Business," *Toledo Blade*, May 18, 2006, p. B1.

Erb, Robin, "Conference at UT Focuses on Prostitution, Sex Trade," *Toledo Blade*, September 30, 2005, p. B3.

―――, "Prostitutes' Plight Prompts Search for Solution," *Toledo Blade,* January 22, 2006, p. A1.

―――, "Workers Needed to Find, Help Prostitutes," *Toledo Blade*, January 27, 2006, p. A1.

―――, "Pimps' Seized Property Eyed as Restitution—Goal Is Aiding the Exploited," *Toledo Blade*, May 26, 2006, p. B1.

―――, "Trafficking in Humans Examined at Meeting—Research Takes Look at Toledo, Columbus," *Toledo Blade*, June 21, 2006, p. B1.

Hall, Christina, "Prostitution Enforcement Among Objectives for '06," *Toledo Blade,* February 17, 2006. p. B5.

Smith, Ryan E., "UT Researcher Has Ideas to Put Oldest Profession Out of Business," *Toledo Blade*, September 7, 2003, p. A1.

Fact Patterns of Concrete Human-Trafficking Cases

In this appendix, we present the fact patterns for the 15 concrete cases.

Case 1

The "Innocence Lost" case involves four grand juries, at least 10 victims, and 31 offenders and seems to be a large part of the reason that human trafficking in Ohio has become a significant public concern.

The case was announced by the U.S. Attorney General, who described a sex-trafficking ring that operated in Ohio, Michigan, Indiana, Illinois, Arkansas, Virginia, Georgia, Maryland, Tennessee, Pennsylvania, California, Florida, Louisiana, and the District of Columbia, where teens were rotated among motels, truck stops, and highway welcome centers. Thirty-one men and women were indicted on charges that included sex trafficking in children, taking minors across state lines for prostitution, conspiracy, racketeering, and money laundering.

Although this case was not centered in Toledo or even in Ohio, it quickly became clear that Toledo residents were many of the victims and offenders in this case. In the initial set of arrests, at least 12 men and two women were among those Toledo residents listed as defendants. One assistant U.S. attorney involved in the case said that the operation involved no fewer than 10 girls forced into prostitution over a four-year period and that most of the girls were from Toledo.

If convicted, the defendants could face up to life in prison, $250,000 in fines for each conviction, and up to $1 million in forfeitures. Although the trials had yet to be completed in this case at the time of this study, one of the coconspirators, a 27-year-old Toledo man, was sentenced to 40 years in federal prison. He pleaded guilty to six federal charges, including conspiracy to engage in interstate transportation of minors for criminal sexual activity, sex trafficking of a minor, and tampering with a witness, victim, or informant.

Case 2

This case involves the kidnap, rape, beating, and sex trafficking of a 14-year-old girl from Michigan. With the help of a female trucker who let a young girl enter her truck, the girl escaped a life of forced sex less than three weeks after her abduction. The victim went out with her 19-year-old boyfriend for her 14th birthday. She thought they were going to the movies but instead they spent several days moving among various homes in Toledo and Michigan. This is where they met the boyfriend's relatives and friends, including a man and woman who soon became her captors. The male, a one-time Toledo resident, promised to take the girl home. Instead, he took her to Indiana and Pennsylvania where he beat and twice raped her and forced her to prostitute herself at various truck stops. The woman, a 22-year-old prostitute, reportedly "trained" the teen in the ways of prostitution.

The male offender was charged and convicted of kidnapping and sex trafficking. He was sentenced to 25 years in federal prison. The female offender pled guilty to sex trafficking. She will serve 46 months in federal prison.

Case 3

This case involves the kidnap and forced trafficking of young girls abducted off a busy Toledo street by a man and a woman. The victims in this case are two girls, cousins ages 14 and 15. The girls entered the car voluntarily and were taken for Chinese food and then back to a Toledo house where an alarm system was set and they were not permitted to leave. The Toledo residents, a 40-year-old man and two women ages 24 and 19, then separated the cousins and "indoctrinated" them. The cousins were told how to behave and solicit customers.

They were sold for sex at least a dozen times, mostly at Toledo-area hotels. They were given clothes and fake identities. An adult always watched and collected payment. They were beaten when they did not follow the rules.

About 10 days into the ordeal, the cousins were taken to a truck stop near Ann Arbor, Michigan, where one was caught with a trucker. Although the sheriff's deputies could not prove prostitution, they reportedly had a gut feeling that the story the young girl told them was not true. Once she was alone with the officers, she told the truth. They called the FBI and the victim's family. Her family picked her up in Michigan and then attempted to find the other cousin, who they thought was taken back to the Toledo house.

The Michigan detective also called the Toledo Police Department and outlined the case for an officer in there. The two officers spoke four times that day, but the offender's name was an alias and the Toledo detective did not have a full address for the house. This misinformation prevented further investigation.

In the meantime, the parents reached the house. Reports verify that the father made his first call more than 90 minutes before police arrived; 911 logged three more calls from the family, plus numerous appeals from neighbors. The father was so enraged he could not wait any longer. He stormed the house, pretending that he had a gun, and a fight ensued. The other victim was apparently shoved out of a second-story window, and when police arrived a short time later, they broke up the fight and sent the two parents to the hospital and the three offenders to jail.

The case was taken by the U.S. Attorney's Office, which indicted the three adults on two counts of sexual trafficking of children, two counts of interstate transportation of minors for prostitution, and conspiracy.

Case 4

The fourth case involves the arrest and prosecution of an ex-Toledoan who was sentenced in Michigan to 20 to 50 years for sexual conduct with a minor. The offender was convicted 10 prior times for sex-related crimes. In this case, the offender befriended a 15-year-old who had run away from foster care and was living on the streets. He offered the girl food, housing, and drugs and eventually employed her as a prostitute. Three weeks after she began with him, she developed a sexually transmitted disease, was hospitalized, and then transferred to a drug rehabilitation center, where the teenager told authorities about her experiences.

Cases 5–10

As of July 2007, a federal task force in Toledo that involves all levels of law enforcement was investigating six cases involving 60 possible human traffickers. These cases are similar to those sex-trafficking cases described above. Each case reportedly involves juvenile victims, and some also involve adults. The women are reportedly prostituted, often in both Toledo and in nearby states, at conventions, "cathouses," hotels, and truck stops. Law enforcement agencies reportedly watch the trafficking operation for a long time and wait until they have information on the most serious offenders and organizers before making arrests. Sometimes, they wait until the trafficker takes the victims out of state to make arrests. A law enforcement respondent explained that an offender in one case had recently been indicted. The case involves a Toledo-area trafficker who allegedly transported Toledo-area juveniles and adults to conventions in Illinois, Michigan, and Washington, D.C., for prostitution. The arrests were made in Washington, D.C. The trafficker pleaded guilty to five felony charges in U.S. District Court in Toledo. He faces at least five years in prison because of a mandatory sentence for compelling underage prostitution.

Case 11

This case involves numerous Russian immigrants in Columbus on tourist visas who were allegedly forced to clean hotels against their will. The case involved a well-known Russian business and community leader who was awarded a contract to clean hotels. Little more is known about this case except that it was pursued by federal law enforcement.

Cases 12–14

Three similar cases identified by a Columbus-area service provider involve well-respected foreign nationals from countries such as Ethiopia, Eritrea, and Guinea who brought individuals to the United States with the promise of employment as housecleaners or nannies. When they arrived, they were forced to work excessive hours without compensation, were not allowed to leave, and were entirely stripped of their freedoms and rights. At least one was abused physically and sexually.

In one of these cases, the victim escaped when the family went on vacation and left her to be supervised by another family. Another was identified by service providers when she was arrested for allegedly stabbing her captor. Service providers suspect that there are more of these cases but that they are difficult to detect because victims are reluctant to come forward because of the high visibility of their captors, because of language barriers, and because of fear of arrest and deportation. Service providers, themselves, suggest that they are currently not comfortable working with law enforcement on these cases.

Case 15

This case involves a high-ranking community leader from Morocco who brought his wife to Columbus and then enslaved her, taking away her freedom of movement, forcing her to work, and abusing her. The same problems associated with identifying and treating these victims exist as in the cases above.

Constructive Cases for Understanding and Responding to Human Trafficking

The content analysis and key respondent interviews revealed reports of incidents and cases for which there was not sufficient information to verify the existence of human trafficking (see Table D.1).[1] These incidents, including prosecutions of job-fraud rings and brothels fronting as legitimate businesses, are described in this appendix. These case types are worth describing because of their potential connections to human-trafficking cases, because of their discussion in the literature, and because, if they were handled or investigated as possible human-trafficking cases, evidence to prosecute them as such may well be discovered. In addition, they may provide important training and policy lessons.

Brothels Fronting as Legitimate Businesses

There are two case types identified, one involving primarily Asian women and the other Hispanic women. There was significantly more information provided in the analysis about the possible cases of human

---

[1] Some of the respondents did have the feeling that these incidents contained the elements of human trafficking. However, they could not articulate all the elements necessary to qualify the cases under the TVPA definition of human trafficking. With other incidents, such as the potential labor exploitation cases, there is simply not enough information available to verify human trafficking. This does not mean that trafficking did not occur in these cases, just that there was not sufficient information to support it.

Table D.1
Content Analysis and Respondent Summary Results, Constructive Cases

Source	Columbus	Toledo	Total/ Average
Content analysis			
Number of articles identified by search terms	10,428	7,420	17,848
Full-text reviews	310	275	585
Articles relevant to human trafficking	23	41	64
Articles referencing cases constructive for human trafficking	13	4	17
Total cases identified from content analysis	5	2	7
Percentage of key respondents referencing cases constructive for human trafficking	25[a]	21[a]	23
Total additional cases identified from key respondent interviews	1	0	1
Total cases from both sources	6	2	8

[a] n = 3

trafficking involving Asian women than Hispanic women. Both case types are described here and rely on the content analysis and key respondent interviews in each site.

Asian Brothels

The Asian brothel cases are similar and surfaced both in Columbus and Toledo, although there was much more discussion of the issue in Columbus than there was in Toledo. None of the respondents in either of the case study sites was working any cases of this type at the time of the interview, but five or six such cases have been investigated in Columbus from about 2005 to 2007, and respondents there estimate that there are as many as 15 to 20 active brothels operating at any given time. No similar estimates were available in Toledo.

These establishments are known to law enforcement and, after arrests are made, the establishments are often replaced quickly by other, similar establishments, most often spas, clinics, and massage parlors. The numbers of workers involved in the raids spanned from two to nine. These workers ranged in age from 36 to 57. All were reportedly from Asian countries, including Thailand and South Korea, and were reportedly moved throughout the country, to and from places such as Texas, New Jersey, California, Georgia, Kentucky, and Virginia.

Similar characteristics are described by the Polaris Project. It suggests that Korean brothels generally employ from one to 12 women and operate as legitimate businesses such as nail salons, massage parlors, or health spas (Davis, 2006).

In many cases we identified, the brothels were infiltrated by undercover police officers or sheriff's deputies who acted as customers to gain access, paid $60 for a massage, and were asked to pay $60 to $180 or more for sex acts, which were cut short. The individuals patronizing these establishments are reported to be primarily white, middle-class men. These characterizations are also found by the Polaris Project (Davis, 2006).

The organizations can be lucrative. As little as $2,000 and as much as $743,000 in cash was seized in various cases identified in this study. In addition, in one case, federal agents tracked about $1.6 million in credit card sales from three connected businesses.

The charges included engaging in or soliciting prostitution, managing a brothel, engaging in corrupt activity, and promoting prostitution (Davis, 2006). In one case, two Toledo women, a Louisville man, and a Los Angeles man pleaded guilty to a Racketeer Influenced and Corrupt Organizations (RICO) conspiracy, money-laundering conspiracy, interstate travel in aid of racketeering, and interstate transportation for purposes of prostitution.

In many cases, bails are set extremely high, $1 billion in one case, because authorities fear offenders would flee if they could post bail and because offenders "have extensive connections throughout the United States" (DeMartini, 2005).

Despite the significant charges and high bails, it is unclear that the penalties will be severe. One woman whose original bail was set for $1 billion received probation after pleading guilty to four counts of promoting prostitution. Four others requested jury trials, the outcome of which was unknown at the time of this study. Further, those who pleaded guilty to RICO and other charges received relatively minor sentences. The Los Angeles man was sentenced to serve 18 months in prison, and the Louisville offender, who cooperated considerably with authorities, was sentenced to one year of probation, six months of which would be served in home confinement.

There is little information about the victims in these cases—the women who work in the spas. One investigator said that the girls are indentured servants because they live, cook, and sleep there. The girls become beholden to those running the spa, according to one of the prosecutors working one of the cases. They come from Korea and Thailand, are in difficult financial positions, and end up in the spa.

However, investigators also report that the women involved in the busts of some of the spas claim that nobody is being held against their will and that the living conditions are good. One investigator reported that their environment was clean, there was a lot of food, and they had everything they needed. The women claim that there are no fights, that everyone is happy, and that they are free to leave if they have the means and do not turn in the owners to law enforcement.

Given these contradictions, although there may be some elements of force, fraud, or coercion, these could not be verified in the analyses. The Polaris Project suggests that some of the women may be trafficked and some may not (Davis, 2006).

Many in law enforcement consider these networks to be highly organized. One investigator suggested that it functioned similarly to a drug operation, and they seemed to get higher in the operation the more they investigated. Another law enforcement officer called the spas part of an organized crime ring that employs women from other states and foreign countries as prostitutes. Officials also said that businesses such as these appear to be organized and capable of rapidly moving people from location to location. However, other respondents characterized the network of Asian spas that cover as brothels to be more "mom and pop" than mafia.

Law enforcement respondents also said that these cases are difficult to work because they require significant resources with little in terms of outcomes in prosecutions; if there were more complaints or more resources dedicated to the issue, it could be more effectively pursued. The criminal justice response is also apparently burdened by lack of resources and the nature of these businesses, which open as quickly as they are closed. Law enforcement officials believe that the supply of women to work in these establishments is great and that they just move new staff in to replace those who are arrested. In addition, local law enforcement officers report that they do not have the tools or resources to prosecute the owners or ringleaders of these establishments. They arrest the workers on minimal charges, who are later released or flee prior to standing trial. Local law enforcement agencies have no contact with service providers for these individuals.

The victims reportedly do not want to cooperate with investigators, who attempt to question them after they are arrested. They provide vague answers to questions and are consistent in their answers, reporting that they arrived in the United States by plane, arrived at their place of business by taxi, do not know anything about the owners or operators of the establishment, and so on. If they provide a phone number, it is always disconnected. They reportedly have no desire for services or help; they just want to be released. There appears to be no service provider or community response to these individuals in either case study site.

Hispanic Brothels

In Columbus, there may be a connection between "one-stop shops" serving a tightly organized, closed Hispanic community and sex trafficking. In this situation, it is thought that Hispanic men could purchase all their needed supplies and services, including trafficked women, from one proprietor.

This description can also be found in a report prepared by the Polaris Project, which suggests that Hispanic residential brothels are closed systems for first-generation Hispanic males who recently immigrated to the United States (Davis, 2006).

There is also the assertion that trafficked women may work on farms and at other businesses that employ migrant workers. This could not be verified in Columbus and is denied in Toledo by respondents with tight ties to the migrant farm communities. The closed nature of these networks makes information about them difficult to obtain (Davis, 2006).

Job-Fraud Rings

Two cases of possible labor exploitation were identified in our analysis in Columbus. No similar cases could be identified in Toledo. These cases involved two different job-fraud rings.

The first case identified involved a three-state, multimillion-dollar job-fraud ring involving hundreds of illegal immigrants. A Tanzanian-born Columbus resident was charged in federal court of conspiring to employ and harbor illegal immigrants, as well as of mail fraud, wire fraud, and money laundering. The job-fraud ring allegedly provided more than 300 illegal immigrants with false identification, transportation, housing, and payroll tax documents.

The second such ring involved two (Columbus-area) individuals who were accused of producing false paperwork to obtain visas, which they used to bring 167 workers into the country illegally through Texas. The pair charged some or all the workers $400 to $800 each to assist them in coming into the United States through El Paso, Texas. The offenders were charged with mail, wire, Social Security, and visa fraud; making false statements; inducing illegal entry into the United States; and conspiracy. They could receive more than 50 years each if convicted.

There was no information about the illegal immigrants and how, and under what premise, they entered the country. Yet respondents claim it is possible that, in addition to smuggling, trafficking for the purposes of forced labor was underlying these cases.

References

Albanese, Jay, Jennifer Schrock Donnelly, and Talene Kelegian, "Cases of Human Trafficking in the United States: A Content Analysis of a Calendar Year in 18 Cities," *International Journal of Comparative Criminology*, Vol. 4, 2004, pp. 96–111.

Andrees, Beate, and Mariska N. J. van der Linden, "Designing Trafficking Research from a Labour Market Perspective: The ILO Experience," *International Migration*, Vol. 43, Nos. 1–2, January 2005, pp. 55–73.

Bales, Kevin, and Steven Lize, *Trafficking in Persons in the United States: A Report to the National Institute of Justice*, Oxford, Miss.: Croft Institute for International Studies, University of Mississippi, 2005. As of September 24, 2007:
http://www.ncjrs.gov/pdffiles1/nij/grants/211980.pdf

City of Toledo, "State of the City Address," 2006. As of October 16, 2007:
http://www.ci.toledo.oh.us/MayorsOffice/Fromthe22ndFloor/
StateoftheCityAddress/tabid/193/Default.aspx

Clawson, Heather J., Mary Layne, and Kevonne Small, *Estimating Human Trafficking into the United States: Development of a Methodology*, Fairfax, Va.: Caliber, 2006.

Clawson, Heather J., Kevonne M. Small, Ellen S. Go, and Bradley W. Myles, *Needs Assessment for Service Providers and Trafficking Victims*, Fairfax, Va.: Caliber, 2003. As of September 24, 2007:
http://www.ncjrs.gov/pdffiles1/nij/grants/202469.pdf

Columbus Chamber of Commerce, "The City of Columbus," brochure, undated. As of September 24, 2007:
http://www.columbus.org/content/lifestyle/Columbus.pdf

Cwikel, Julie, and Elizabeth Hoban, "Contentious Issues in Research on Trafficked Women Working in the Sex Industry: Study Design, Ethics, and Methodology," *Journal of Sex Research*, Vol. 42, No. 4, November 2005, pp. 306–316.

Davis, Kathleen Y. S., *Human Trafficking and Modern Day Slavery in Ohio*, Washington, D.C.: Polaris Project, February 2006. As of October 11, 2007: http://216.128.14.181/polarisproject/programs_p3/Ohio_Report_Trafficking.pdf

de Baca, L., and A. Tisi, "Working Together to Stop Modern-Day Slavery," *Police Chief*, Vol. 69, No. 8, 2002, pp. 78–80.

de Boer, Roberta, and Robin Erb, "Reports of Runaways End Up at Bottom of Investigation Pile—Lack of Manpower, Parental Interest Deters Probes," *Toledo Blade*, February 12, 2006a, p. A1.

———, "Surviving in Wayne's World," *Toledo Blade*, May 14, 2006b, p. A1.

DeMartini, Alayna, "Brothel Suspect's Bond at $1 Billion; Woman Among Four Charged After Raid on Massage Parlors," *Columbus Dispatch*, June 24, 2005, p. 1B.

DHHS—*see* U.S. Department of Health and Human Services.

DHS—*see* U.S. Department of Homeland Security.

DOJ—*see* U.S. Department of Justice.

DOL—*see* U.S. Department of Labor.

DOS—*see* U.S. Department of State.

Dowling, Samantha, Karen Moreton, and Leila Wright, *Trafficking for the Purposes of Labor Exploitation: A Literature Review*, London, UK: Home Office, 2007. As of September 24, 2007: http://www.homeoffice.gov.uk/rds/pdfs07/rdsolr1007.pdf

Erb, Robin, and Roberta de Boer, "Crackdown Exposes Toledo as a Hub of Teen Prostitution—Local Residents Provide Management, Muscle, Recruits for National Operation," *Toledo Blade,* January 8, 2006a, p. A1.

———, "Harrisburg Area Proved Profitable for Pimps, Prostitutes from Toledo—Arrests, Fines Viewed as Routine Part of Business," *Toledo Blade*, March 19, 2006b, p. A1.

Estes, Richard J., and Neil Alan Weiner, *The Commercial Sexual Exploitation of Children in the United States, Canada and Mexico*, Philadelphia, Pa.: University of Pennsylvania School of Social Work, Center for the Study of Youth Policy, 2001. As of September 24, 2007: http://fl1.findlaw.com/news.findlaw.com/hdocs/docs/sextrade/upenncsec90701.pdf

Farquet, Romaine, Heikki Mattila, and Frank Laczko, "Human Trafficking Bibliography by Region," *International Migration*, Vol. 43, Nos. 1–2, January 2005, pp. 301–342.

Feingold, David A., "Human Trafficking," *Foreign Policy*, September–October 2005, pp. 26–28, 30, 32.

Finckenauer, Jim, and Min Liu, "State Law and Human Trafficking," draft presented at Marshalling Every Resource: State Level Responses to Human Trafficking conference, Princeton University, December, 2006. As of September 24, 2007:
http://www.princeton.
edu/prior/events/conferences/past_events/conference_39.html_1/pub_1_43.pdf

Fossum, Donna, Lawrence S. Painter, Valerie L. Williams, Allison Yezril, Elaine M. Newton, David Trinkle, *Discovery and Innovation: Federal Research and Development Activities in the Fifty States, District of Columbia, and Puerto Rico*, Santa Monica, Calif.: RAND Corporation, MR-1194-OSTP/NSF, 2000. As of October 10, 2007:
http://www.rand.org/pubs/monograph_reports/MR1194/

GAO—*see* U.S. Government Accountability Office.

GlobalSecurity.org, "Defense Supply Center Columbus (DSCC)," Web page, August 21, 2005. As of October 18, 2007:
http://www.globalsecurity.org/military/facility/columbus-dd.htm

Gozdziak, Elzbieta M., and Elizabeth A. Collett, "Research on Human Trafficking in North America: A Review of Literature," *International Migration*, Vol. 43, Nos. 1–2, January 2005, pp. 99–128.

Hoemann, Warren, "Remarks of Warren Hoemann, Deputy Administrator, Federal Motor Carrier Safety Administration, to the Toledo Transportation Club," speech delivered at the Annual Election Dinner, May 18, 2005. As of September 24, 2007:
http://www.fmcsa.dot.gov/about/news/speeches/ttc-051805.htm

Human Smuggling and Trafficking Center, "Distinctions Between Human Smuggling and Human Trafficking," fact sheet, Washington, D.C.: U.S. Department of State, January 2005. As of September 24, 2007:
http://www.usdoj.gov/crt/crim/smuggling_trafficking_facts.pdf

Jahic, Galma, and James O. Finckenauer, "Representations and Misrepresentations of Human Trafficking," *Trends in Organized Crime*, Vol. 8, No. 3, March 2005, pp. 24–40.

Landesman, Peter, "The Girls Next Door," *New York Times Magazine*, January 25, 2004, p. 30.

Miko, Francis T., *Trafficking in Persons: The U.S. and International Response*, Washington, D.C.: Congressional Research Service, 2006.

Minnesota Statistical Analysis Center, *Human Trafficking in Minnesota: A Report to the Minnesota Legislature*, St. Paul, Minn.: Minnesota Office of Justice Programs, 2006. As of September 24, 2007:
http://www.dps.state.mn.us/OJP/cj/publications/Reports/2006_Human_Trafficking.pdf

National Institute of Justice, "International Human Trafficking Research," undated Web page. As of September 25, 2007:
http://www.ojp.usdoj.gov/nij/international/programs/inttraffick.html

Newman, Graeme R., *The Exploitation of Trafficked Women*, Washington, D.C.: Center for Problem-Oriented Policing, Problem Specific Guides Series, No. 38, 2006. As of September 24, 2007:
http://www.cops.usdoj.gov/mime/open.pdf?Item=1699

Public Law 106-386, Victims of Trafficking and Violence Protection Act of 2000, October 28, 2000.

Public Law 109-13, Emergency Supplemental Appropriations Act for Defense, the Global War on Terror, and Tsunami Relief, 2005, May 11, 2005.

Pyle, Encarnacion, "Columbus Becoming a Mini Melting Pot," *Columbus Dispatch*, March 14, 2006, p. 1A.

Raymond, Janice G., and Donna M. Hughes, *Sex Trafficking of Women in the United States: International and Domestic Trends*, New York: Coalition Against Trafficking in Women, 2001. As of September 24, 2007:
http://action.web.ca/home/catw/attach/sex_traff_us.pdf

Richard, Amy O'Neill, *International Trafficking in Women to the United States: A Contemporary Manifestation of Slavery and Organized Crime*, Washington, D.C.: Central Intelligence Agency, Center for the Study of Intelligence, 1999. As of September 24, 2007:
https://www.cia.gov/library/center-for-the-study-of-intelligence/csi-publications/books-and-monographs/trafficking.pdf

Ridgeway, Greg, Terry Schell, K. Jack Riley, Susan Turner, and Travis L. Dixon, *Police-Community Relations in Cincinnati: Year Two Evaluation Report*, Santa Monica, Calif.: RAND Corporation, TR-445-CC, 2006. As of October 10, 2007:
http://www.rand.org/pubs/technical_reports/TR445/

Riley, K. Jack, Susan Turner, John MacDonald, Greg Ridgeway, Terry Schell, Jeremy M. Wilson, Travis L. Dixon, Terry Fain, Dionne Barnes-Proby, and Brent D. Fulton, *Police-Community Relations in Cincinnati*, Santa Monica, Calif.: RAND Corporation, TR-333-CC, 2005. As of October 10, 2007:
http://www.rand.org/pubs/technical_reports/TR333/

Schauer, Edward J., and Elizabeth M. Wheaton, "Sex Trafficking into the United States: A Literature Review," *Criminal Justice Review*, Vol. 31, No. 2, June 2006, pp.146–169.

"Study: Columbus Has Ohio's Best Economy," *Business First of Columbus*, August 28, 2006. As of October 16, 2007:
http://columbus.bizjournals.com/columbus/stories/2006/08/28/daily21.html

Sturm, Roland, William Goldman, and Joyce McCulloch, "Mental Health and Substance Abuse Parity: A Case Study of Ohio's State Employee Program," Santa Monica, Calif.: RAND Corporation, RP-754, 1999. As of October 10, 2007:
http://www.rand.org/pubs/reprints/RP754/

Taylor, Mark, "Interview Regarding Domestic Servitude (Segment One)," U.S. Department of State, Washington, D.C., 2007. As of September 24, 2007:
http://www.state.gov/g/tip/rls/rm/07/81704.htm

Tyldum, Guri, and Annette Brunovskis, "Describing the Unobserved: Methodological Challenges in Empirical Studies on Human Trafficking," *International Migration*, Vol. 43, Nos. 1–2, January 2005, pp. 17–34.

UN—*see* United Nations.

United Nations, *Protocol to Prevent, Suppress, and Punish Trafficking in Persons, Especially Women and Children, Supplementing the United Nations Convention Against Transnational Organized Crime,* General Assembly resolution 55/25, 2001. As of September 24, 2007:
http://www.ohchr.org/english/law/protocoltraffic.htm

U.S. Attorney General's Office, *Attorney General's Annual Report to Congress on U.S. Government Activities to Combat Trafficking in Persons, Fiscal Year 2005,* Washington, D.C.: U.S. Department of Justice, 2006. As of September 24, 2007:
http://www.usdoj.gov/ag/annualreports/tr2005/agreporthumantrafficing2005.pdf

U.S. Census Bureau, "Columbus (City) QuickFacts from the U.S. Census Bureau," 2007a. As of September 24, 2007:
http://quickfacts.census.gov/qfd/states/39/3918000.html

———, "Toledo (City) QuickFacts from the U.S. Census Bureau," 2007b. As of September 24, 2007:
http://quickfacts.census.gov/qfd/states/39/3977000.html

U.S. Department of Health and Human Services, "Look Beneath the Surface: Human Trafficking Is Modern-Day Slavery," undated Web page. As of September 24, 2007:
http://www2.acf.hhs.gov/trafficking/index.html

U.S. Department of Homeland Security, "Human Trafficking and Human Smuggling," Web page, May 2, 2006. As of September 25, 2007:
http://www.ice.gov/pi/investigations/publicsafety/humantrafficking.htm

U.S. Department of Justice, "What We Do: Fight Trafficking in Persons," undated Web page. As of September 25, 2007:
http://www.usdoj.gov/whatwedo/whatwedo_ctip.html

———, *Assessment of U.S. Government Activities to Combat Trafficking in Persons in Fiscal Year 2005,* Washington, D.C., 2006. As of September 24, 2007:
http://www.usdoj.gov/ag/annualreports/tr2006/assessment_of_efforts_to_combat_tip.pdf

————, *Attorney General's Annual Report to Congress on U.S. Government Activities to Combat Trafficking in Persons for Fiscal Year 2006,* Washington, D.C., 2007. As of September 27, 2007:
http://www.usdoj.gov/ag/annualreports/tr2006/agreporthumantrafficing2006.pdf

U.S. Department of Labor, "Office of Child Labor, Forced Labor, and Human Trafficking (OCFT)," undated Web page. As of September 25, 2007:
http://www.dol.gov/ilab/programs/ocft/

U.S. Department of State, "Office to Monitor and Combat Trafficking in Persons," undated Web page. As of September 25, 2007:
http://www.state.gov/g/tip/

————, *Trafficking in Persons Report, June 2006*, Washington, D.C., 2006. As of September 24, 2007:
http://www.state.gov/g/tip/rls/tiprpt/2006/

U.S. Government Accountability Office, *Human Trafficking: Better Data, Strategy, and Reporting Needed to Enhance U.S. Antitrafficking Efforts Abroad*, Washington, D.C., July 2006. As of September 24, 2007:
http://www.gao.gov/new.items/d06825.pdf

U.S. Statutes, Title 36, Section 825, White Slave Traffic Act, June 25, 1910.

Wilson, Deborah G., William F. Walsh, and Sherilyn Kleuber, "Trafficking in Human Beings: Training and Services Among US Law Enforcement Agencies," *Police Practice and Research*, Vol. 7, No. 2, May 2006, pp. 149–160.